OVER
1500
FANTASTIC
JOKES

Written and compiled by Guy Campbell & Mark Devins
Illustrated by Paul Moran & Simon Ecob

First published in Great Britain in 2002 as three separate books
(*The World's Funniest Animal Jokes for Kids, The World's Funniest School
Jokes for Kids* and *The World's Funniest Disgusting Jokes for Kids*)
by Dean.

This edition published in Great Britain in 2002 by Dean,
an imprint of Egmont Books Limited,
239 Kensington High Street,
London W8 6SA

ISBN 0 681 19173 2

Printed and bound in Singapore

3 5 7 9 10 8 6 4

PART ONE
ANIMAL JOKES

**What do Paddington, Rupert and Pooh
pack when they go on holiday?**
Just the bear essentials!

How do you get six donkeys in a fire engine?
Two in the front, two in the back and
two on the top going "Heehaw Heehaw
Heehaw"!

**What do you get if you cross a centipede
and a chicken?**
Enough drumsticks to feed an army!

**A man walks into a pub with a tiger.
"Do you serve Welsh people in here?"
he asks the barman.
"Certainly, Sir." the barman replies.**
"Good. A pint for me, then, please, and two
Welsh people for the tiger..."

**What happened when the chef found a daddy
long legs in the salad?**
It became a daddy short legs!

What do ants take when they're ill?
Anty Biotics!

What is a newly hatched beetle?
A baby buggy!

A little turtle begins to climb a tree slowly. After long hours of great effort, he reaches the top, jumps into the air, waving his front legs frantically, then crashes heavily into the ground. After recovering consciousness, he starts to climb the tree again, jumps once more, but again crashes to the ground. The little turtle does this again and again, while all the time his heroic efforts are being watched with sadness by a couple of birds perched on a nearby branch. Finally, the female bird says to the male bird, "Dear, don't you think it's time to tell Tommy he is adopted?"

What do you get if you cross a glow worm with a python?
A 15-foot strip light that can strangle you to death!

Where did Noah keep his bees?
In the ark hives!

What do you call a vet with laryngitis?
A hoarse doctor!

How do you change tyres on a duck?
With a quackerjack!

What does Tarzan say when he sees a herd of elephants in the distance?
"Look, a herd of elephants in the distance!"

What does Tarzan say when he sees a herd of elephants wearing sunglasses in the distance?
Nothing. He doesn't recognise them!

Why shouldn't you take bears to the zoo?
Because they'd rather go to the cinema!

**What noise does a cat make
going down the motorway?**
Miaoooooooooooooooooooooooooooooooooow!

**What is the difference between a flea-bitten
dog and a bored visitor?**
One's going to itch and the other
is itching to go!

**Hickory dickory dock,
the mice ran up the clock.
The clock struck one,**
the rest got away with minor injuries!

**A penguin walks into a bar and
says to the barman,
"Have you seen my Dad?"
"I don't know," says the barman.**
"What does he look like?"

A man and his dog sat in a movie hall, both enjoying a movie. When the film ended, the dog applauded until his paws were sore. The man sitting on the next seat was wonderstruck.
"That's amazing!" he exclaimed.
"Yes, it is," agreed the dog owner.
"He hated the book..."

What do you get if you cross a cat with a parrot?
A carrot!

What's big, grey and mutters?
A mumbo jumbo!

Where do monkeys make toast?
Under a gorilla!

How do we know elephants are always unhappy?
Because of their great sighs!

How do bees get to school?
By school buzz!

Last time David went to the zoo he got into trouble for feeding the monkeys...
He fed them to the lions!

What do you call a woodpecker with no beak?
A headbanger!

What is green, sooty and whistles when it rubs its back legs together?
Chimney Cricket!

Where do you weigh a whale?
At the whale-weigh station!

What do you call a vampire's dog?
A werewoof!

What do you get if you cross a skunk with a boomerang?
A horrendous smell that keeps coming back!

A duck walks into a pharmacy and says "Got any bread?" The pharmacist explains he has no bread because it is a pharmacy. Then he tells the duck to try the supermarket nearby. Fifteen minutes later the duck comes back and says, "Got any bread?" The pharmacist again tells the duck he doesn't sell bread and to try another shop around the corner. A few minutes later the duck is back again and says, "Got any bread?" The pharmacist screams that if the duck asks him for bread one more time he will nail its bill to the floor. The duck leaves. Twenty minutes later the duck comes back. "Got any nails?" he says. The pharmacist explains that **NO**, being a **PHARMACIST**, he doesn't sell **NAILS** either. "Oh," says the duck, "in that case... Got any bread?"

What do you get if you cross a tiger with a kangaroo?
A stripey jumper!

A baby blackbird fell out of its nest and went flying through the branches of the oak tree towards the ground.
"Are you all right?"
called out a magpie as the chick went hurtling past his perch.
"So far!" said the little bird.

What do Alexander the Great and Winnie-the-Pooh have in common?
They both have "the" as their middle names!

A tortoise is mugged one day by a gang of snails. The police asked him what his attackers looked like and he said,
"I really don't know, it all happened so fast!"

What's black, yellow and covered in blackberries?
A bramble bee!

What has ten guns
and terrifies the ocean?

Billy the squid!

What has six legs, four ears, two trunks and three tusks?
An elephant with spares!

What's brown and sees just as well from either end?
A horse with its eyes shut!

Why do elephants have grey skin?
To keep their insides from falling out!

Why aren't elephants allowed on beaches?
They can't keep their trunks up!

Why did they make two Yogi Bears?
Because they made a Boo-Boo with the first one!

What do you get if you cross an elephant with the abominable snowman?
A jumbo yeti!

What has antlers and sucks blood?
A moose-quito!

What's grey and wrinkled and lights up?
An electric elephant!

What did one centipede say to the other centipede?
You've got a lovely pair of legs, you've got a lovely pair of legs, you've got a lovely pair of legs, you've got a lovely pair of legs...!

What did the bee say to the naughty bee?
Bee-hive yourself!

Why do elephants have big ears?
Because Noddy wouldn't pay the ransom!

A man goes into a pet shop and asks to buy a wasp. The shopkeeper tells him they don't sell wasps. "That's strange," says the man.
"You had one in the window yesterday!"

**What does a caterpillar do on
New Year's Day?**
Turns over a new leaf!

Which fly makes films?
Stephen Speilbug!

**What's pretty, delicate and carries a
machine-gun?**
A killer butterfly!

**Why didn't the two worms get on
Noah's Ark in an apple?**
Because everyone had to go on in pears!

**What do you get if you cross a fish
and a Ducati?**
A motor pike!

Why don't centipedes play football?
Because by the time they've got their boots
on, it's time to go home!

What wears glass slippers and weighs a ton?
Cinderelephant!

A Shaggy Dog Story

A local business looking for office help put a sign in the window saying: "HELP WANTED. Must be able to type, must be good with a computer and be bilingual". A short time later, a dog trotted up to the window, saw the sign and went inside. He looked at the receptionist and wagged his tail, then walked over to the sign, looked at it and whined. Getting the idea, the receptionist got the office manager. The office manager looked at the dog and was surprised, to say the least. However, since the dog looked determined, he led him into the office. Inside, the dog jumped up on the chair and stared at the manager, who said, "I can't hire you.

You have to be able to type."
The dog jumped down, went to the typewriter and typed out a perfect letter. He took out the page and trotted over to the manager, gave it to him and then jumped back on the chair. The manager was stunned, but then reminded the dog, "The sign says you have to be good with a computer." The dog jumped down again and went to the computer. He then demonstrated his expertise with various programs, producing a sample spreadsheet and database. By this time, the manager was totally dumbfounded! He looked at the dog and said, "I realise that you are a very intelligent dog and have some fantastic abilities. However, I still can't give you the job. The sign also says that you have to be bilingual."
The dog looked him straight in the face, and said, "Meow."

What do you call a camel with three humps?
Humphrey!

Why is a baseball team like fish and chips?
They both need a decent batter!

What do you get when you put a fish and an elephant together?
Swimming trunks!

What has four wheels and flies?
A wheelie bin!

What do you call a cow with no sense of direction?
Udderly lost!

What do you get if you cross a skunk with an elephant?
A smell you never forget!

What do you get if you cross a cow with a crystal ball?

A message from the udder side!

How do snails get their shells so shiny?
Snail varnish!

Why did the fly fly?
Because the spider spied 'er!

How can you get a set of teeth put in for free?
Smack a lion!

If a four-legged animal is a quadruped and a two-legged animal is a biped, what's a tiger?
A stri-ped!

What do you call a lion who has eaten your mother's sister?
An aunt-eater!

What do you get if you cross a rabbit and a flea?
Bugs Bunny!

Why do sea-gulls fly over the sea?
Because if they flew over the bay
they would be bagels!

**What do you get if you cross a toad
with a mist?**
Kermit the Fog!

What do insects learn at school?
Mothematics!

How do you start a bug race?
One, two, flea - go!

**What is the difference between a flea
and a wolf?**
One prowls on the hairy and the other howls
on the prairie!

**What happened at the badly organised cow
milking contest?**
It was udder chaos...

How do fleas travel?
Itch hiking!

What kind of key opens a banana?
A monkey!

What is a myth?
A female moth!

**A salesman dropped in to see
a business customer.
No one was in the office except
a big dog emptying wastebaskets.
The salesman stared at the animal,
wondering if his imagination could
be playing tricks on him.
The dog looked up and said,
"Don't be surprised. This is just part of
my job." "Incredible!" exclaimed the man.
"I can't believe it! Does your boss
know what a prize he has in you,
an animal that can talk?"**

"Don't tell him that!" said the dog.
"If he finds out I can talk, he'll make me answer the phone as well!"

Why were the flies playing football in a saucer?

They were playing for the cup!

Why can't two elephants go swimming?

Because they have only one pair of trunks between them!

A Polar Bear cub says to his mum: "Mum, are you sure I'm a Polar Bear?" "Yes, of course, Darling. Why would you ask me that?" The little bear says:

"Because I'm absolutely FREEZING!"

What do worms leave round their baths?

The scum of the earth!

When is the best time to buy budgies?

When they're going cheap!

What do butterflies sleep on?

Caterpillows!

What did the earwig skydiver say as it jumped out of the plane?

Earwig go!

What is the definition of a caterpillar?
A worm in a fur coat!

**How come if ants are always
so busy they always get
time to show up at picnics?**

What is smaller than an ant's mouth?
An ant's dinner!

**What do you get if you cross a
pony and a detective?**
Inspector Horse!

What says "Quick, Quick"?
A duck with hiccups!

What's green and loud?
A froghorn!

What is a little dog's favourite drink?
Pupsi-cola!

A crab is sitting on the ocean floor when a lobster comes up to him dragging a half-dead octopus. The octopus is coughing, very pale and has a nasty rash.
The lobster says to the crab:
"Alright, mate, here's that sick squid
I owe you."

What does a flamingo do when it rains?
It gets wet!

What do you call a pony with a sore throat?
A little horse!

Why did the dolphin cross the beach?
To get to the other tide!

What do ducks watch on TV?
Duckumentaries!

What do whales eat?
Fish and ships!

Why did the crab get arrested?
Because he was always pinching things!

Why wouldn't they let the butterfly into the dance?
Because it was a moth ball!

What do you get when you cross a parrot with a monster?
A creature that gets a cracker whenever it asks for one!

It was a boring Sunday afternoon in the jungle so the Elephants decided to challenge the Ants to a game of soccer. The game was going well with the Elephants beating the Ants ten goals to nil, when the Ants gained possession. The Ants' star player was dribbling the ball towards the Elephants' goal when the Elephants' left back came lumbering towards him.

The Elephant trod on the little Ant, killing him instantly. The referee stopped the game. "What the hell do you think you're doing? Do you call that sportsmanship, killing another player?" The Elephant replied, "Well, I didn't mean to kill him...

I was just trying to trip him up!"

Why did the parrot wear a raincoat?
Because she wanted to be Polly
unsaturated!

**What did the gamekeeper say to the
lord of the manor?**
"The pheasants are revolting!"

When does a cart come before a horse?
In the dictionary!

**How does a queen bee get
around her hive?**
She's throne!

**What do you get if you cross a dinosaur
with a dog?**
Tyrannnosaurus Rex!

**What kind of snack do little monkeys
have with their milk?**
Chocolate chimp cookies!

This kangaroo escaped his enclosure at London Zoo. After recapturing the kangaroo, the zookeeper put up a ten-foot fence round the enclosure. Next morning, the kangaroo was out again, roaming around the zoo. So the fence was extended to 20 feet high. Next morning, sure enough, the kangaroo is out again. Frustrated, the zoo officials built the fence 40 feet high. A camel in the next enclosure asked the kangaroo, "Gee, how much higher do you think they'll go?" The kangaroo said, "About a 1,000 feet I guess, unless somebody starts locking the gate..."

What does a queen bee do when she burps?
Issues a royal pardon!

What do whales like to chew?
Blubber gum!

Where does Duck Lightyear go?
To infinity, and the pond!

What do horses play when they're bored?
Stable tennis!

What do you call a bee born in May?
A maybe!

Two escaped lions are walking through a city centre. One says:
"Quiet today, isn't it?"

What do parrots eat?
Polyfilla!

What's the difference between a worm and an apple?
Have you ever tried worm pie?

There was an old man in France who used to get up every morning at five a.m. He would then go and sprinkle a white powder on the roads. When a passing policeman asked him

what he was sprinkling on the roads, he answered that it was elephant powder. The policeman scoffed, "But everybody knows that there are no elephants in France!" and the old man said,

"You see, it works!"

What did one worm say to the other when he was late home?
Where in earth have you been?

What kind of doorbell do bees have?
A hum dinger!

Why are elephants wrinkly?
Because they hate being ironed!

**A snake says to his Mother,
"Mum, am I poisonous?"
"Why do you ask, love?" says his Mum.**
"I've just bitten my tongue!"

What happened when the cat swallowed a coin?
There was some money in the kitty!

**Customer: This fish isn't cooked.
Waiter: How do you know?**
Customer: It's eaten all my chips!

What happens when it rains cats and dogs?
You step in a poodle!

How do you start a teddy bear race?
Ready, teddy, go!

What do you give a sick budgie?
Tweetment!

What goes hum-choo, hum-choo?
A bee with a cold!

Why do elephants have trunks?
Because they would look silly with glove compartments!

Why did the turtle cross the road?
To get to the Shell garage!

What should you do if you are suddenly chased by a big pink bird?
Flamin' Go!

Why did the chicken cross the playground?
To get to the other slide!

What goes "Hith Hith"?
A snake with a lisp!

What's black and white and makes a lot of noise?
A zebra with a drum kit!

Why don't elephants wear shoes?
They can't tie the laces on their back feet when they have shoes on their front feet!

What goes zzub, zzub?
A bee flying backwards!

What did the bee say to the other bee in summer?
Swarm here isn't it?

What do you call a cat that has just eaten a whole duck?

A duck-filled fatty puss!

A frog goes to see a fortune teller and is told, "You are going to meet a beautiful young girl who will want to know everything about you."
The frog says, "This is great! Will I meet her at a party, or what?"
"No," says the psychic.
"In her biology class."

How did Bo Peep lose her sheep?
She had a crook with her!

Why don't elephants like turnips?
For the same reasons that people don't like turnips!

What's the difference between a fish and a piano?
You can't tuna fish!

What do you call a pig with three eyes?
A piiig!

What happens when geese land in a volcano?
They cook their own gooses!

How do you find where a flea has bitten you?
Start from scratch!

What did the teddy bear say to the waiter when he offered him some pudding?
No thanks. I'm stuffed!

Have you ever seen a man-eating tiger?
No, but in the café next door I once saw a man eating chicken!

What is a Twip?
It's when wabbits twavel!

What's the difference between a rabbit that runs and a rabbit that goes "Kalaka Hoo Ha!"
One's a fit bunny and the other's a bit funny!

Customer: When I bought this cat, you told me he was good for mice. He won't go near them!
Shopkeeper: Well, isn't that good for mice?

What do you get from a drunk chicken?
Scotch eggs!

What does a bee get at McDonalds?
A humburger!

Which side of a chicken has the most feathers?
The outside!

Why don't elephants wear high heels?
They think they already have pretty ankles!

What do you get if you cross a cow with a grass cutter?
A lawn mooer!

What do you get when giraffes collide?

A giraffic jam!

What insect is good for you?
Vitamin bee!

How can you tell if an elephant is getting ready to charge?
He pulls out his American Express card!

What looks like half a cat?
The other half!

What do you call a big Irish spider?
Paddy long legs!

What do you call a bald teddy?
Fred bear!

Why are igloos round?
So penguins can't hide in the corners!

How do you know when there's an elephant under the bed?
Your nose is touching the ceiling!

What is green and pecks on trees?
Woody Wood Pickle!

Why did the bees go on strike?
They wanted more honey and
shorter flowers!

**How can you tell if an elephant has used
your toothbrush?**
It smells of peanuts!

**What happened when the boy jellyfish
met the girl jellyfish?**
Jelly babies!

What goes 99-clonk, 99-clonk, 99-clonk?
A centipede with a wooden leg!

**What do you call a rabbit wearing a
blue and white scarf?**
A Chelsea Bun!

Upon entering the little village shop, a tourist noticed a sign saying "DANGER! BEWARE OF DOG!" posted on the glass door. Inside he noticed a harmless old hounddog asleep on the floor beside the cash register. He asked the shop manager, "Is that the dog folks are supposed to beware of?" "Yep, that's him," the manager replied.
The stranger looked amused.
"That old thing? He's got no teeth and he must be 35 years old! Why in the world would you put up a sign saying 'Danger! Beware of the dog'?" "Because," the owner replied, "before I put that sign up, people kept tripping over him."

How can you tell if you are looking at a police glow worm?
It has a blue flashing light!

The Tramp and the Hamster

A tramp goes into a restaurant and orders a burger. The waiter says, "No way. I don't think you can pay for it." The tramp says, "You're right. I don't have any money, but if I show you something you have never seen before, will you give it to me?" The waiter agrees, and the tramp reaches into his pocket, and pulls out a hamster. The hamster runs to the end of the counter, climbs down to the floor, runs across the room, and gets up on to the piano and starts playing Elton John tunes. The waiter says, "Wow, that hamster is a really good piano player!" He brings the tramp a burger, which he eats, and he asks for another. "Money or another miracle," says the waiter. The tramp reaches into his coat again and pulls out a frog. He puts the frog on the counter, and the frog starts to sing Ricky

Martin songs brilliantly. A stranger from the other end of the counter runs over to the tramp and offers him a hundred pounds for the frog. The tramp says, "OK", and takes the money. The stranger takes the frog and runs out of the restaurant. The waiter says, "Are you crazy? You've just sold a singing frog for a hundred pounds? It must have been worth millions!"

"Nah," says the guy. "The hamster is also a ventriloquist."

What's more dangerous than being with a fool?
Fooling with a bee!

What do you get if you cross a cat with a canary?
Shredded tweet!

What do you call a Russian flea?
A Moscow-ito!

What do you get if you cross an elephant with a whale?
A submarine with a built-in snorkel!

What were the only creatures not to go into the Ark in pairs?
The maggots, they went in an apple!

If you get referees in football and umpires in tennis, what do you get in bowls?
Goldfish!

What time is it when an elephant sits on your fence?
New fence time!

What would you do if an elephant sat in front of you at the movies?
Miss most of the film!

What do you get if you cross a shark with a parrot?
An animal that talks your head off!

What wobbles and eats peanuts?
Jelly the Elephant!

What's grey, has a wand, huge wings and gives money to elephants?
The tusk fairy!

Why do you need a licence for a dog and not for a cat?
Cats can't drive!

What's worse than raining cats and dogs?
Hailing taxis!

Why did the cat join the Red Cross?
Because she wanted to be a first-aid kit!

Why did Mickey Mouse get shot?
Because Donald Ducked!

What do polar bears have for lunch?
Ice burgers!

How does a bird with a broken wing manage to land safely?
With a sparrowchute!

What do bees chew?
Bumble gum!

Why did the muddy chicken cross the road twice?
He was a dirty double crosser!

What do you call a cheerful frog?
A hop-timist!

Why did the cat sleep under the car?
Because she wanted to wake up oily!

What is the difference between a fly and a bird?
A bird can fly but a fly can't bird!

What should you give a nervous elephant?
Trunquillizers!

Waiter, there's a fly in my soup!
What do you want for 85p, an ostrich?

What book tells you all about chickens?
A hencyclopaedia!

How do you make a statue of an elephant?
Take a piece of rock and carve away everything that doesn't look like an elephant!

The Brave Pig

A man is visiting a farm when he notices a pig with only three legs. When he meets the farmer, he asks him how the pig came to be so disabled.

"That pig is a marvel," said the farmer, "an absolute gem. He once saved my chickens from a couple of foxes! He heard a noise one night and saw the foxes about to get through the fence and scared them off by banging a wooden spoon on a bucket." "That's amazing," said the man. "Did the foxes bite off his leg?" "No, no," said the farmer, "I tell you, that pig is worth his weight in gold. He once stopped burglars robbing my house. We were all out in the village one day and armed burglars broke into the house. He dialled 999 and let the tyres down on their car. The police caught them and recovered all our stuff." "Good Lord!" said the man. "But tell me, how did he lose the leg?

continued overleaf

Did the burglars shoot him?" "No, no, no," said the farmer, his eyes filling with tears, "I tell you, that pig is an angel sent from above. Do you know he saved my daughter's life? She was only six years old and she fell asleep in the barn one evening while feeding the new lambs with their bottle by lamplight. The lamp fell over and set fire to some hay, and before you know it the whole place was in flames. That pig went into the blazing barn and pulled my daughter out. Then he went back in eight more times and rescued every single lamb as well!" "Incredible!" said the man. "And he lost his leg in the fire?" "No, no, no," said the farmer. "THEN HOW DID HE LOSE HIS LEG?!" said the exasperated man.

"Well," said the farmer, "when you have a pig as truly exceptional as that... you don't want to eat him all at once, do you?"

Kenya

There were four cats in a boat, one jumped out. How many were left?
None. They were all copy cats!

What did one flea say to the other after a night out?
Shall we walk home or take a dog?

What is worse than finding a maggot in your apple?
Finding half a maggot!

What's got eight legs and can fly long distances?
Four geese!

What do you call a flea on the moon?
A lunar-tick!

What do you give an elephant that's going to be sick?
Plenty of space!

What is the difference between a cat and a comma?
One has the paws before the claws and the other has the clause before the pause.

What do you get if you cross a parrot with a centipede?
A walkie-talkie!

What chases the Roadrunner and sings disco pop tunes?
Kylie Coyote!

Where do birds meet for coffee?
In a nest-café!

What do you call a crate of ducks?
A box of quackers!

What is a parrot's favourite game?
Hide and Speak!

What happens when a bomb goes off in the middle of a herd of cows?
Udder destruction!

How can you tell which end of a worm is which?
Tickle it in the middle and see which end laughs!

What is the best advice to give to a worm?
Sleep late!

What is an asset?
A small donkey!

Two hunters find some tracks in the forest.
"Those are bear tracks," said one.
"No way, those are moose tracks," said the other.
And then they were run over by a train...

What do you get if you cross an elephant and a kangaroo?

Great big
holes all
over
Australia!

Harry was trying to smuggle a skunk out of America to sell it abroad; he asks his friend the best way to do it. "Just stick it down your trousers," his friend said. "He won't bite unless you sit on him." "But what about the terrible smell?" said Harry. His friend thought for a moment. "He'll get used to it eventually!"

What is out of bounds?
A knackered kangaroo!

What did the bee say to the flower?
Hi honey!

What do you get if your budgie flies into the blender?
Shredded Tweet!

How do you start a firefly race?
Ready Steady Glow!

What did the spider say to the bee?
Your honey or your life!

What do cows play at parties?
Moo-sical chairs!

The Mighty Tiger

A tiger corners a monkey one day and roars: "WHO IS THE MIGHTIEST OF ALL THE JUNGLE ANIMALS?" The poor monkey replies: "You, of course! No-one is mightier than you, Tiger!" A little while later the tiger finds a deer, and bellows out: "WHO IS THE MIGHTIEST OF ALL THE JUNGLE ANIMALS?" The deer is shaking so hard it can barely speak, but manages to squeak: "Oh Great Tiger, you are the mightiest animal in the jungle!" The tiger, feeling good, swaggers up to a female elephant that is quietly eating some weeds. He roars: "WHO IS THE MIGHTIEST OF ALL THE JUNGLE ANIMALS?" The elephant grabs the tiger with her trunk, slams him down, picks him up again, and shakes him until his teeth rattle. Finally she throws him hard into a nearby tree. The tiger staggers to his feet and looks at the elephant and says: "Just because you don't know the answer, you don't have to get so upset..."

What happens when ducks fly upside down?
They quack up!

What's grey on the inside and clear on the outside?
An elephant in a plastic bag!

What do frogs eat with their hamburgers?
French flies!

Why do elephants wear sandals?
To keep from sinking into the sand!

Why do ostriches stick their heads in the sand?
To look for elephants that weren't wearing sandals!

What happened to the hyena that swallowed an Oxo cube?
He made a laughing stock of himself!

What did the woodworm say to the chair?
It's been nice gnawing you!

What happened when the owl lost his voice?
He didn't give a hoot!

What do you get when you cross a python with a porcupine?
Ten feet of barbed wire!

What do you call a cat who does tricks?
A magic kit!

How do you get two whales in a Nissan Micra?
Straight up the M4 and over the Severn Bridge. (To Wales.)

How do you get four elephants in a Nissan Micra?

Two in the front, two in the back!

How do you recognise an elephant's house?

There's a Nissan Micra outside!

Two monkeys had a dare, to paint a lion's bottom blue as he slept. Bobby monkey crept up to the sleeping beast and carefully painted its hindquarters, but suddenly the lion woke up. Bobby shot off like a hare, being chased by the angry lion. Through the jungle they sped, until Bobby jumped over the wall to a house. Quickly, he sat in a garden chair and pulled a newspaper over his face. The enraged lion wasn't far behind: he came leaping over the wall and stopped in front of the trembling monkey. "Did you see a monkey come through here?" said the lion. "What?" said Bobby, still shaking. "The one that painted that lion's bum blue?"

"Oh no!" said the lion. "Don't tell me it's in the papers already!"

How do you make an elephant stew?
You keep it waiting for a few hours!

How can you tell an elephant from a giraffe?
Say "Hi giraffe" and if it doesn't answer, it's probably an elephant!

I went to the dentist yesterday. He said, "Say Aaah." I said, "Why?"
He said, "My dog's died."

What looks like a horse and flies?
A flying horse!

Who clucked and conquered half the world?
Attila the Hen!

What did the buffalo say when his son went on holiday?
Bison!

How do you find out how many cows you have?
With a pocket cowculator!

What part of a fish weighs the most?
The scales!

What did the banana do when the monkey chased it?
The banana split!

Farmer Brown meets his friend in the village pub. "Harold, what did you give your bull when it had colic?" "Vinegar and Fairy Liquid," said Harold. A week later they met again. Farmer Brown says, "Oi, Harold! I gave my bull vinegar and Fairy Liquid, like you said, and it died!"
"So did mine!" said Harold.

Which dinosaur had one leg?
All of them!

What do you get when you cross a cow and a duck?
Cheese and quackers!

Why don't owls sing when it is raining?
Cos it's too wet to woo!

The Rude Parrot 2

A lady was walking to work and she saw a parrot on a perch in front of a pet shop. The parrot shouted,"Oi! You're really ugly!" Well, the lady was furious! She stormed past the shop to her work. Going home that night, she saw the same parrot and it said, "Oi! You're really ugly!" She was very angry. She went into the shop and told the owners that she was going to sue them and have the bird put down if they didn't make it stop insulting her. The owners told her they would make sure he didn't do it again. The next morning, she again passed in front of the shop. The parrot was still on his perch. When she walked by, the parrot said, "Oi!" She stopped and turned to the parrot and said, "Yes, what?"

The parrot looked at her and said:
"You know..."

What is white, sugary, has whiskers and floats?
A catameringue!

What did the slug say as he slipped down the wall?
How slime flies!

What is the difference between fleas and dogs?
Dogs can have fleas but fleas can't have dogs!

What did the clean dog say to the insect?
Long time no flea!

What goes clomp, clomp, clomp, squish; clomp, clomp, clomp, squish?
An elephant with one wet shoe!

What happened when 500 hares got loose on the main street?
The police had to comb the area!

A vicar was reading Bible stories
to his Sunday school class. He read:
"The man named Lot was warned to
take his wife and flee out of the city,
but his wife looked back
and was turned into a pillar of salt."
One of the children asked,
"What happened to the flea?"

**What became of the man who was
swallowed by a cow?**
He became the man in the moo!

What do you give a dog with a fever?
Mustard, it's the best thing for a hot dog!

Why do baby giraffes walk softly?
Because they can't walk hardly!

What does an elf get in a cow field?
A pat on the head!

What do you get if you cross a pig and a laundry?

Hogwash!

Teacher: If I gave you three rabbits today and five rabbits tomorrow, how many rabbits would you have?
Jackie: Nine.
Teacher: That's not right, you'd have eight.
Jackie: No, I'd have nine. I already have one rabbit at home!

What did the fish say when he swam into the wall?
Dam!

What do you call a story about young horses?
A pony tail!

Why don't you see elephants in lifts?
Because they hide in the back corners!

Why do elephants drink so much?
To try to forget!

A vicar is buying a parrot.
"Are you sure it doesn't scream, yell, or swear?" asked the preacher.
"Oh absolutely. It's a religious parrot," the shopkeeper assured him. "Do you see those strings on his legs? When you pull the right one, he recites the Lord's Prayer, and when you pull on the left he recites the 23rd Psalm." "Wonderful!" says the preacher. "But what happens if you pull both strings?"
"I fall off my perch, you fool!" screeched the parrot.

Two fleas were running across the top of a cereal packet.
"Why are we running so fast?" said one.
"Because it says 'Tear along the dotted line!'"

Why should you never buy dogs that are going cheap?
Because a healthy dog should go "Woof"!

The Talking Dog

A man and his dog walk into a bar.
The man says to the barman:
"I'll bet you a round of drinks that my
dog can talk." The bartender says, "Yeah!
Sure...go ahead." The man says to his
dog, "What covers a house?" and his dog
says, "Roof!" The man says, "How does
sandpaper feel?" and the dog says,
"Rough!"
The man asks, "What percentage of the
Earth's surface is water?"
and the dog says, "Arf!"
"There!" said the man.
"I told you he could talk!"
The bartender, annoyed at this point,
throws both of them out the door.
Sitting on the pavement,
the dog looks at the man and says,
"Or is it three-quarters?"

What's big, white and scary with a hole in the middle?

A polo bear!

What do you get if you cross a frog with a traffic warden?
Toad away!

Why did King Kong climb the Empire State Building?
Because he couldn't fit in the lift!

What's pink and grey and has four feet?
A hippopotamus poking its tongue out!

Rachel: How did you like the parrot I sent you?
Michele: It was delicious!
Rachel: You ate it? I paid 500 dollars for that parrot, and it spoke seven different languages!
Michele: Then why didn't it say anything when I put it in the oven?!

Who took ten thousand pigs up a hill?
The Grand Old Duke of Pork!

Who steals soap from the bath?
Robber ducks!

A magician was working on a cruise ship performing tricks for the guests. But his act was ruined every night by the captain's parrot, who would shout out, "It's up your sleeve!" or "She's gone through the hidden trapdoor!" during his act, and give the tricks away. Unfortunately, the ship struck an iceberg one night and the magician and the parrot ended up in the same lifeboat. After a week of silence, the parrot turned to the magician and said,

"All right, I give up - what did you do with the ship?"

What should you do if you are on a picnic with King Kong?

Give him the biggest bananas!

How do you stop a cockerel crowing on Sunday morning?

Have him for lunch on Saturday!

The Antique Saucer

A famous art collector is walking through the city when he notices an old cat lapping milk from a saucer in the doorway of a shop.
He notices that the saucer is extremely old and very, very valuable.
So he walks casually into the store and offers to buy the cat for £2. The shopkeeper replies, "I'm sorry, but the cat isn't for sale."
The collector says, "Please, I need a hungry cat around the house to catch mice.
I'll pay you £20 for him."
And the shopkeeper says, "Sold!" and hands over the cat. The collector continues,
"Hey, for the 20 quid I wonder if you could throw in that old saucer? The cat's used to it and it'll save me from
having to get a dish."
And the shopkeeper says,
"Sorry, Mate, but that's my lucky saucer.
So far this week I've sold 68 cats!"

**What happened when the cat ate
a ball of wool?**
She had mittens!

**Customer: I'll take this parrot. Could you
please send me the bill?**
Shopkeeper: I'm sorry, but you'll have to
take the whole bird!

**What do you get when you cross a pig
and a centipede?**
Bacon and legs!

**A Ring-Tailed Lemur goes into a tea shop
and orders a jam scone.
"That'll be £2.50 please, Sir,"
said the waitress.
"I must say, we don't get many
Ring-Tailed Lemurs in here!"**
"I'm not surprised," said the Lemur.
"Two and a half quid for a scone?!"

What's grey and squirts jam at you?
A mouse eating a doughnut!

What do you get if you pour boiling water down a rabbit hole?
Hot cross bunnies!

What has six ears, twelve legs and can't watch telly?
Three blind mice!

The Bragging Horses

Some racehorses are chatting in a stable.
One of them starts to boast
about his track record: "In the last 15
races I've run, I've won 8 of them!"
"That's nothing!" another horse breaks in,
"In the last 27 races I've run, I've won
19!" "Oh that's not bad," says
another, flicking his tail,
"but in the last 36 races I've run,
I've won 28!"
At this point, they notice that a
greyhound dog has been sitting
there listening. "I don't mean to boast,"
says the greyhound,
"but in my last 104 races,
I've won 103 of them."
The horses are clearly amazed.
"Wow!" says one, after a hushed silence.
"A talking dog!"

Why does an ostrich have such a long neck?
Because its head is so far from its body!

How can you tell when your dog is stupid?
He keeps barking up the wrong tree!

What do giraffes have that no other animal has?
Baby giraffes!

My dog likes to sit down each evening and surf the Internet.
Wow! What a smart animal!
Not really, it took the cat three weeks
to teach him!

What do we get from naughty cows?
Bad milk!

Why did the dinosaur cross the road?
Because chickens weren't invented then!

What do you get if you cross a cow and a jogging machine?
A milk shake!

A Chihuahua, a Doberman and a Bulldog are in a doggie bar having a drink when a good-looking girl Poodle comes up to them and says, "Whoever can say 'liver and cheese' in the best sentence can go out on a date with me." So the Doberman says, "I love liver and cheese." The Poodle says, "That's not good enough!" The Bulldog says, "I hate liver and cheese." She says, "That's not good enough either!"
Finally, the Chihuahua says, "Liver alone... cheese mine!"

How do you stop an elephant from going through the eye of a needle?
Tie a knot in its tail!

Why did the ram run over the cliff?
He didn't see the ewe turn!

What's the loudest pet you can have?
A trumpet!

The Escaped Gorilla

A gorilla escapes from the zoo and after three weeks, the zoo keepers give up looking for him. Some time later, a man calls the zoo complaining of a gorilla in a tree in his back yard. The zoo keeper rushes right over. When he arrives, he has a net, a baseball bat, a shotgun, and a huge dog. The man asks what the items are for. He's told, "I'm gonna climb the tree and hit the gorilla in the head with the baseball bat. When he falls out of the tree, you throw the net over him. The dog will go straight for his bum and bite it really hard." The man asks, "But what's the shotgun for?" The zoo keeper answers, "If I miss the gorilla and fall out of the tree, you shoot the dog..."

What goes dot-dot-dash-dash-squeak?
Mouse code!

A guy went into a police station and put a dead cat on the counter. "Somebody threw this into my front garden!" he complained. "Alright, sir," said the officer.
"Come back in six months and if no-one's claimed it, it's yours!"

What did the giant canary say?
TWEET!

What do greedy fish eat?
Everyfin!

What has six legs and flies?
An airline pilot with a cat!

What does a cat go to sleep on?
A caterpillar!

Why was night cricket invented?
Because bats like to sleep in the daytime!

Why did the turkey cross the road?
It was the chicken's day off!

The Jungle Violinist

A famous violinist is canoeing up a river in Africa when he hits a rock and is forced to swim for shore. Soon he is surrounded by 40 hungry, snarling jungle beasts, from tigers and hyenas to huge man-eating snakes. The animals advance towards the musician, drooling. Thinking quickly, he whips out his violin and begins to play.
Sure enough, the animals are so bewitched by the music that they stop snarling and sit down to listen.
Presently an old crocodile emerges from the river, shuffles straight up to the violinist and eats him.

"Hey!" said a lion, "What are you doing? We were enjoying that!"

"PARDON?!" says the crocodile...

A woman is thinking about buying a mink coat. "Will it be all right in the rain?" she asked the shop assistant.
"Have you ever seen a mink with an umbrella?" he said.

Two sheep meet on a country lane. The first one says, "Baa!" The second one says, "Woof!" "What are you up to? Sheep don't go 'Woof'." said the first sheep.
"I'm sorry," said the second, "I'm new round here."

Why did the antelope?
Nobody gnu!

Why did the pelican refuse to pay for his meal?
His bill was too big!

What always goes to bed with shoes on?
A horse!

Tony, who lives in the city, asks a farmer: "Why doesn't this cow have any horns?"
Farmer: "There are many reasons: some cows are born without horns, some cows shed their horns, some cows have their horns taken out. But as for this cow here, the reason is simple. It's a horse."

What do you get if you cross a road with a safari park?
Double yellow lions!

A girl finds a frog in the woods. "Excuse me, young lady," says the frog, "I'm not really a frog, I'm a Prince! Kiss me and you will return me to my real form!" "No thanks," said the girl.
"Princes are two a penny, but a talking frog? I'm going to make a packet!"

How do lobsters travel around?
Taxi crab!

How do you teach a dog to fetch?
Tie a cat to a stick!

What did the triceratops wear on its legs?
Tricerabottoms!

Why did the Tyrannosaurus stand in the corner?
Because he'd been naughty!

What lies on the ground 100 feet up in the air?
A dead caterpillar!

A bloke goes into a pub with a giraffe, they both get drunk and the giraffe collapses in a heap on the floor. The bloke goes to leave and the barman says, "Hey! You can't leave that lying on the floor!"
The bloke says:
"It's not a lion, it's a giraffe."

A Tasmanian wide-mouthed frog

This joke requires the teller to make two special faces!

The toad's speaking face.

The punch-line face.

Once, a Tasmanian wide-mouthed frog decided to leave Tasmania and see the world. After a long journey over land and sea, he found himself in Africa...

continued overleaf

Everything was new and exciting to him, and he was full of questions. He met a giraffe and said, "Wow! You're so tall, what are you?" "I'm a giraffe," said the giraffe. "Hello! I'm a Tasmanian wide-mouthed frog! What do giraffes eat?" said the Tasmanian wide-mouthed frog. "Oh, I eat leaves and fruit, mainly," said the giraffe. The frog said goodbye and hopped off. Next he came across a zebra. "Wow!" he said. "A stripey horse!" "No. I'm a zebra," said the zebra. "Hello! I'm a Tasmanian wide-mouthed frog! What do zebras eat?" said the Tasmanian wide-mouthed frog. "Oh, I eat grass, mainly," said the zebra. The frog said goodbye and hopped off. Soon, he came upon a great, big lion. "Wow!" said the Tasmanian wide-mouthed frog. "What are you?!" "I'm a lion," said the lion.

"Wow!" said the frog. "And what do lions eat?" The lion looked him right in the eye. "We eat Tasmanian wide-mouthed frogs," said the lion. "Oh..," said the frog,

"I don't suppose you get many of those round here, do you?"

Two guys are out hiking. All of a sudden, a bear starts chasing them. They climb a tree, but the bear starts climbing up the tree after them. The first guy gets his trainers out of his knapsack and starts putting them on. The second guy says, "What are you doing?" He says: "I figure when the bear gets close to us, we'll jump down and make a run for it." The second guy says: "Are you crazy? You can't run faster than a bear!" The first guy says: "I don't have to run faster than the bear. I only have to run faster than you!"

Baby skunk: Can I have a chemistry set for my birthday?
Mummy Skunk: No.
Baby Skunk: Why not?
Mummy Skunk: Because I don't want you stinking the house out!

What's grey, yellow, grey, yellow, grey, yellow, grey, yellow, grey, yellow, grey, yellow?
An elephant rolling down a hill with a daisy in its mouth.

What do you call it when a frog takes a shower?
Spring cleaning!

**A horse, a monkey, a vicar, an Englishman, an Irishman, a Scotsman, a Rabbi, a hamster, a clown and a blonde all walk into a bar together.
The barman turns to them and says:**
"Is this some kind of a joke?"

A naughty young chick is being told off by his angry Mum.
"If your father could see you now," said Mother Hen, "he'd turn over in his gravy!"

A fireman is working on the engine outside the station when he notices a little girl next door in a little red wagon with little ladders hung off the side and a garden hose tightly coiled in the middle. The girl is wearing a fireman's helmet and has the wagon tied to a dog and cat. The fireman walks over to take a closer look. "That's a nice fire engine," the fireman says with admiration. "Thanks," the girl says. The fireman looks a little closer and notices the girl has tied the wagon to the dog's collar and to the cat's tail. "Excuse me, Miss," the fire fighter says, "I don't want to tell you how to run your fire engine, but if you were to tie that rope around the cat's collar, I think you could go faster." The little girl replied, "You're probably right, but then I wouldn't have a siren."

What kind of ties do pigs wear?
Pig stys!

A man goes into a pet shop and tells the owner that he wants to buy a pet that can do everything. The shop owner suggests a faithful dog. The man replies, "Come on, a dog?" The owner says, "How about a cat?" The man replies, "No way! A cat certainly can't do everything. I want a pet that can do everything!" The shop owner thinks for a minute, then says, "I've got it! A centipede!" The man says, "A centipede? I can't imagine a centipede doing everything, but okay... I'll try a centipede." He gets the centipede home and says to the centipede, "Clean the kitchen." Thirty minutes later, he walks into the kitchen and... it's immaculate! All the dishes have been washed, dried, and put away; the counter-tops cleaned; the appliances sparkling; the floor waxed. He's amazed. He says to the centipede, "Clean the living room."

Twenty minutes later, he walks into the living room. The carpet has been vacuumed; the furniture cleaned and dusted; the pillows on the sofa plumped; the plants watered.

The man thinks to himself, "This is the most amazing thing I've ever seen. This really is a pet that can do everything!" Next he says to the centipede, "Run down to the corner and get me a newspaper." The centipede walks out the door. Ten minutes later... no centipede. Twenty minutes later... no centipede. Thirty minutes later... no centipede. By this point the man is wondering what's going on. The centipede should have been back in a couple of minutes. Forty-five minutes later... still no centipede! So he goes to the front door, opens it ... and there's the centipede sitting right outside. The man says, "Hey! I sent you down to the corner shop 45 minutes ago to get me a newspaper. What's the matter?!"

The centipede says, "I'm goin'! I'm goin'! I'm just puttin' on my shoes!"

What would you get if Batman and Robin were run over by a herd of stampeding elephants?
Flatman and Ribbon!

What does it mean when the Easter Bunny arrives one day late with melted chocolate?
He probably had a bad hare day.

Why do hens lay eggs?
If they dropped them, they'd break!

A leopard went to see an optician because he thought he needed an eye exam. "Every time I look at my wife," he worriedly told the optician, **"I see spots before my eyes." "So what's to worry about?" replied the doctor. "You're a leopard, aren't you?"**
"What's that got to do with anything?" replied the patient. "My wife is a zebra!"

Two fish were in a tank.
One says to the other,
"So, how do you drive this thing?"

It's a sunny morning in the Big Forest and the Bear family are just waking up. Baby Bear goes downstairs and sits in his small chair at the table.
He looks into his small bowl. It is empty!
"Who's been eating my porridge?!" he squeaks. Daddy Bear arrives at the table and sits in his big chair. He looks into his big bowl. It is also empty!
"Who's been eating my porridge?!" he roars. Mummy Bear puts her head through the serving hatch from the kitchen and screams,
"For Pete's sake, how many times do we have to go through this? I haven't made the stupid porridge yet!"

How does a rabbit make gold soup?
He begins with 24 carrots.

What did the frog order at McDonald's?
French flies and a diet Croak!

A mother and baby camel are talking one day when the baby camel asks, "Mum, why have I got these huge three-toed feet?" The mother replies, "Well son, when we trek across the desert your toes will help you to stay on top of the soft sand." "OK," said the son. A few minutes later the son asks, "Mum, why have I got these great long eyelashes?" "They are there to keep the sand out of your eyes on the trips through the desert." "I see," replies the son. After a short while, the son returns and asks, "Mum, why have I got these great big humps on my back?" The mother, now a little impatient with the boy replies, "They are there to help us store water for our long treks across the desert, so we can survive without eating and drinking for long periods of time!" "That's great, Mum, so we have huge feet to stop us sinking, and long eyelashes to keep the sand from our eyes and these humps to store water, but Mum..." "What now!?"

"Why are we in London Zoo?"

**How does a frog feel when he has
a broken leg?**
Very unhoppy!

**How do you hide an elephant
in a box of Smarties?**
Paint his toenails all different colours!

**Hank heard a shot, followed by howling
and another shot.
He ran next door and found
his friend Tony crying.
"Say, what's wrong?" Hank asked.
Tony sobbed, "I had to shoot my dog."
Hank said, "My God! Was he mad?"**
Tony replied,
"Well, he wasn't too happy about it."

**A country dog, coming to the city and
seeing his first parking meter, thinks,**
"How do you like that? Pay toilets!"

What did the duck say when he'd finished shopping?
Put it on my bill please!

How do you keep an elephant from stampeding?

Take his stampeder away!

One night, two vampire bats were hanging upside down in a cave. One says, "Hey, you wanna go and get some blood?" and the other bat says, "Where are we going to get blood at two in the morning?"

So the other bat says, "You don't want to go? Fine, I'll go by myself!"

And off he flapped. About 30 minutes later, the first bat came back with fresh blood dripping out of his mouth and all over his body.

The second bat says, "Hey, where did you get all that blood?"

The first bat says, "See that tree over there?"

"Yeah," says the second bat..

"Well I didn't," said the first bat.

PART TWO
SCHOOL JOKES

Teacher: Tommy, put some more water in the fish tank...
Pupil: Why, Miss? I put some in only yesterday and he hasn't drunk that yet!

Billy: Do you think it's right to punish people for things they haven't done?
Teacher: No, Billy, of course not.
Billy: Good. I haven't done my homework!

Mum, I got 100 in an arithmetic test and still didn't pass!
Why not, for goodness sake?
Because the answer was 200!

Our teacher talks to herself. Does yours?
Yes, but she doesn't realise it, she thinks we're actually listening!

Teacher: You missed school yesterday didn't you?
Pupil: Not very much, no!

Mother: How was school today?
Lisa: OK, but our teacher doesn't really know what she's doing.
Mother: What makes you think that?
Lisa: Well, today she told us that four and four makes eight.
Mother: That's right!
Lisa: But yesterday she said that six and two makes eight!

Teacher: What are the small rivers that run into the Nile?
Pupil: The juve-niles!

Jono: My grandad is still living at 103.
Teacher: Amazing, 103 years old!
Jono: No, 103 Station Road!

Teacher: If you add 3452 and 3096, then divide the answer by 4 and multiply by 6, what would you get?
Tony: The wrong answer!

What's purple and ruled the world?
Alexander the Grape!

"Bobby, I have read your essay about your house," said the teacher, **"and it's word for word exactly the same as your brother's from last year!"**
"Of course it is," says Bobby.
"It's exactly the same house!"

Why did the student eat his homework?
The teacher told him it was a piece of cake!

Why did the germ cross the microscope?
To get to the other slide!

Pupil: If a person's brain stops working, does he die?
Teacher: You're alive, aren't you?

How can you tell a Geomet Tree?
It has square roots!

When does five and five make eleven?
When you're stupid!

Teacher: What are you writing?
Pupil: A letter to myself.
Teacher: What does it say?
Pupil: I don't know. I won't get it till tomorrow.

Why isn't whispering permitted in class?
Because it's not aloud!

Teacher: Why do they say the pen is mightier than the sword?
Pupil: Because no one's invented a ballpoint sword yet!

Teacher: Dorothy, what did you write your report on?
Dorothy: A piece of paper!

Mother: How was your first day at school?
Son: It was all right except for some man called "Teacher" who kept spoiling all our fun!

What are you going to be when you get out of school?
An old man!

Pupil: My teacher was mad with me because I didn't know where the Lake District was.

Mother: Well, next time, remember where you put things!

Jack: I'm not going back to school ever again.
Jim: Why ever not?

Jack: The teacher doesn't know a thing, all she does is ask questions!

Fred came home from his first day at school. "Nothing exciting happened," he told his mother,

"except the teacher didn't know how to spell 'cat', so I had to tell her."

I'm really glad you called me Fred, Dad.
Why is that?

Because when I got to school that's what everybody else called me!

Teacher: If you had five apples on your desk and the boy next to you took three what would you have?
Pupil: A fight!

Dad, can you help me find the lowest common denominator in this problem please?
Don't tell me that they haven't found it yet: I remember looking for it when I was a boy!

The teacher was doing counting with her first year class. "Jackie," she asked, "can you count to 10 without mistakes?" "Yes," said Jackie, and she did. "Now, Fred," said the teacher, "can you count from 10 to 20?"
"That depends," said Fred, "with or without mistakes?"

Teacher: The word 'politics' - can you give me an example of how to use it?
Pupil: My parrot swallowed a watch and now Polly ticks!

My teacher reminds me of history.
She's always repeating herself!

A nursery school teacher was observing her classroom of children while they drew pictures. She would occasionally walk around to see each child's artwork. As she got to one little girl who was working quietly, she asked what the drawing was of. The girl replied, "I'm drawing God." The teacher paused and said, "But no one knows what God looks like." Without looking up from her drawing the girl replied, "They will in a minute."

**Teacher: Class, we will have only half a day of school this morning.
Class: Hooray!**
Teacher: We will have the other half this afternoon!

**Pupil (on phone): My son has a bad cold and won't be able to come to school today.
School Secretary: Who is this?**
Pupil: This is my father speaking!

Teacher: Why were you late?
Henry: Sorry, Miss, I overslept.
Teacher: You mean you sleep at home too?

Teacher: That's quite a cough you have there, what are you taking for it?
Jules: I don't know Miss.
What do you think it's worth?

Father: How do you like going to school?
Son: The going bit is fine, and the coming home bit too, but I'm not too keen on the time in between!

Teacher : Fred, your ideas are like diamonds.
Fred: You mean they're so valuable?
Teacher: No, I mean they're so rare!

Teacher: "You're pretty dirty, Helen."
Helen: "You should see me when I'm clean. I'm even prettier!"

**Teacher:
When do
astronauts eat?**
Pupil: At launch time!

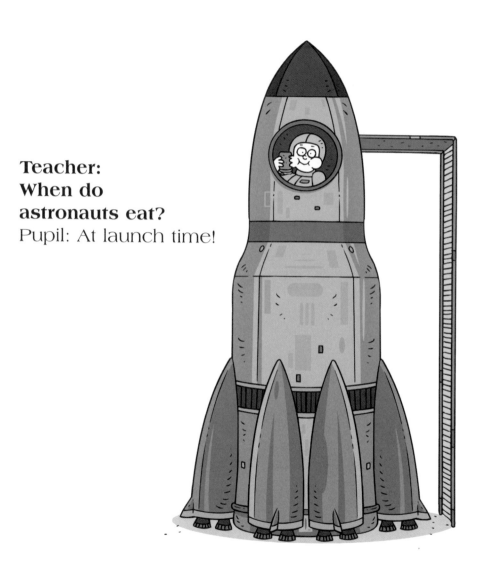

The Spanish explorers went round the world in a galleon.
Really? How many galleons did they get to the mile?

What did King Henry V say when he got on his horse at the battle of Agincourt?
Giddy up!

Teacher: What is migration?
Tim: A headache birds get when they fly south for the winter!

Why aren't you doing very well in history?
Because the teacher keeps asking about things that happened before I was born!

Dad: How did you do in your tests?
Son: I did what Winston Churchill did.
Dad: What was that?
Son: I went down in history!

"Is ink very expensive, Dad?"
"No, son, what makes you ask that?"
"Well, I spilt some on the Headmaster's carpet, and he went bananas!"

Teacher: Is Lapland heavily populated?
Class: No, there are not many Lapps to the mile!

The mathematics teacher saw that Johnny wasn't paying attention in class.
She called on him and said,
"Johnny! what are 6, 9, 28 and 44?"
Johnny quickly replied:
"Sky One, The Disney Channel, Granada Breeze and Cartoon Network!"

Dean: I didn't do my homework because I lost my memory.
Teacher: Goodness! When did this start?
Dean: When did what start?

Teacher: What are you reading?
Pupil: I dunno!
Teacher: But you're reading aloud!
Pupil: But I'm not listening!

Fred: I've added these figures ten times.
Teacher: Good work!
Fred: And here are my ten answers!

Father: What did you learn in
school today?
Son: That three and three are seven.
Father: Three and three are six!
Son: In that case I didn't learn
anything today!

Teacher: Why was George Washington
buried at Mount Vernon?
Pupil: Because he was dead!

Teacher: What comes before 7?
Frank: The postman?

Teacher: Why do animals have fur coats?
Caroline: Because they would look stupid in denim jackets?

Teacher: Name three famous poles?
Mary: North, south and tad!

Father: I hear you skipped school to play football.
Son: No I didn't, and I have the fish to prove it!

Teacher: I'd like to go through one whole day without having to tell you off.
Pupil: You have my permission!

Teacher: Julie, take 932 from 1,439. What is the difference?
Julie: That's what I say, what's the difference?

Teacher: Why are you the only one in class today?
Pupil: Because I missed school dinner yesterday?

Why does your geography exam have a big zero over it?
It's not a zero, the teacher ran out of stars, so she gave me a moon instead!

If I had five coconuts and I gave you three, how many would I have left?
I don't know.
Why not?
In our school we do all our arithmetic in apples and oranges!

What did you learn in school today?
Not enough, they want me to go back tomorrow!

Teacher: If I lay one egg here and another there, how many eggs will there be?
Fred: None!
Teacher (surprised): Why not?
Fred: I don't think you can lay eggs!

Teacher: What is an island?
Kev: A piece of land surrounded by water except on one side.
Teacher: On one side?
Kev: Yes, the topside!

"It's perfectly clear," said the teacher, "that you haven't studied your geography. What's your excuse?"
"Well, my dad says the world is changing every day. So I decided to wait until it settles down!"

Teacher: I said to draw a cow eating some grass but you've only drawn the cow?
Pupil: Yes, the cow ate it all!

Mother: Does your teacher like you?
Son: Like me, she loves me! Look at all those X's she put on my homework!

Teacher: If I had seven apples in one hand and eight apples in the other, what would I have? Student: Massive hands!

Teacher: What can you tell me about the Dead Sea?
Pupil: Dead? I didn't even know it was sick!

Teacher: What birds are found in Portugal?
Pupil: Portu-geese!

What animal is best at mathematics?
Rabbits, they multiply the quickest!

"Our teacher has a bad memory. For three days she asked us how much is two and two. We told her it was four. But she still hasn't got it.
Today she asked us again!"

Name an animal that lives in Lapland -
A reindeer.
Good, now name another.
Another reindeer!

Teacher: What's 2 and 2?
Pupil: 4
Teacher: That's good.
Pupil: Good? That's perfect!

The class had settled down to its colouring books. Stevie came up to the teacher's desk and said, "Miss Brownin', I ain't got no crayons." "Stevie," Miss Browning said, "you mean, 'I don't have any crayons. You don't have any crayons. We don't have any crayons. They don't have any crayons.' Do you see what I'm getting at?"
"You're jokin'!" Stevie said, "Who's 'ad all the crayons?"

Teacher: How can you prove the world is round?
Pupil: I didn't say it was!

Do you ever get straight A's?
No, but I sometimes get dodgy B's!

Teacher: This note from your father looks like your handwriting.
Pupil: Well, yes, he borrowed my pen!

Teacher: Would you at the back of the room stop passing notes?
Pupil: We're not passing notes. We're playing poker!

Are you in the top half of your class?
No, I'm one of the students who make the top half possible!

Elena's teacher was quizzing them on the alphabet. "Elena," she says, "what comes after 'O'?"
Elena says, "Yeah!"

Teacher: Spell "bet".
Ronan: B-e-t-t.
Teacher: Leave one of the t's.
Ronan: Which one?

What computer comes with the best chips?
A big Mac!

Jeff: My Gran knitted me three socks for my birthday...
Belinda: Why three socks?
Jeff: Because I wrote to her that I'd grown another foot!

Police arrested two children, one for drinking battery acid and the other one for eating fireworks.
They charged one and let the other one off!

What happens to a hamburger that misses a lot of school?
He has a lot of ketchup time!

What do elves do after school?
Gnomework!

Teacher: What's the biggest thing ever made from fruit?
Jill: The grape wall of China!

What was Camelot?
It's the place where people
used to park their camels!

Grandad: When I was your age, I could name all the kings and queens of England...
Grandson: Yes, but there hadn't been so many of them then!

Why were the teacher's eyes crossed?
She couldn't control her pupils!

Why don't cannibals like mathematics?
Because when you add four and four you get ate!

Dad: Come on, son, finish your homework, a little hard work never killed anyone...
Son: Well, I don't want to be the first!

Teacher: What family does the Antelope belong to?
Dawn: I don't know, nobody in our street's got one!

What would happen if you took the school bus home?
The police would make you bring it back!

Teacher: Simon, can you spell your name backwards?
Simon: No Mis!
Teacher: Tony, can you spell your name backwards?
Tony: Yes, Y not!

One day, Ella says to her Mum, "I've been banned from cooking classes." Mum asks why. "Because I burnt something."
"And what did you burn?" said Mum.
"The school."

What did the pencil say to the rubber?
Take me to your ruler!

Why do people go to night school?
So they can learn to read in the dark!

One day during cooking class, the teacher, Mrs. Jones, was telling the class her secrets for making perfect sauces. When she ordered them to the cookers to start cooking, she said, "And don't forget to use wooden spoons." As Donna stirred her sauce, she thought about the physics behind the mystery of the wooden spoon and decided it must have something to do with heat conduction. She approached Mrs. Jones to test her theory. "Why do we use wooden spoons, Miss?" she asked. "Because," she replied, "if I had to sit here listening to all your metal spoons banging against the metal pots all afternoon, I'd go mental."

Teacher: What did Julius Caesar say to Brutus when Brutus stabbed him?

Emma: Ow!

Teacher: Name four members of the cat family.

Pupil: Daddy cat, mummy cat and two kittens!

Teacher: If I bought a hundred currant buns for a pound, what would each bun be?

Pupil: Stale!

Son: I'm not going back to school tomorrow!
Father: Why not?

Son: Well, I've been there a whole day, I can't read, I can't write and they won't let me talk, so what's the point?

Mother: How do you like your new teacher?

Son: I don't. She told me to sit up the front for the present and then she didn't give me one!

Mother: What was the first thing you learned in class?

Daughter: How to talk without moving my lips!

One day a college professor of Psychology was greeting his new college class. He stood up in front of the class and said, "Would everyone who thinks he or she is stupid please stand up?" After a minute or so of silence, a young man stood up. "Well, hello there. So you actually think you're an idiot?" the professor asked. The kid replied, "No sir, I just didn't want to see you standing there all by yourself."

Teacher: Where are you from, Pascal?
Pascal: I am from France, Miss.
Teacher: That's nice, which part exactly?
Pascal: All of me is from France.

Teacher: What's Fred's other name?
Jack: Fred who?

Teacher: If I cut two oranges into seven pieces, what have I got?
Francine: Sticky fingers!

Teacher: In 1940, what were the Poles doing in Russia?

Pupil: Holding up the telephone wires!

Lee comes home from school one day with a huge black eye. His Mum is suitably annoyed. "Not again!" she says. "How many times have I got to tell you, if you think you're going to lose your temper, stop and count to ten before you get into some silly fight!" "I did!" said Lee.

"But Jack Thomson's Mum told him to count only to five..."

Teacher: Why did Stone Age man draw cave pictures of rhinoceroses and hippopotamuses?

Tony: Because he didn't know how to spell them!

149

Mother: Son, what do you think of your new teacher?
Son: He's okay, but a bit strict.
Mother: What do you mean strict?
Son: Well, he thinks that words can be spelt only one way!

Teacher: How can you make so many mistakes in just one day?
Pupil: I get up early!

Teacher: What time do you wake up in the morning?
Pupil: About an hour and a half after I get to school!

Father: Well, Son, how are your exam results?
Son: They're under water.
Father: What do you mean?
Son: Below "C" level!

Son: Dad, can you write with your eyes shut?
Dad: Course I can.
Son: Good. Can you sign my report card?

Teacher: Why are you so late?
Tony: Well, I was obeying the sign that says 'School Ahead, Go Slow'.

Bobby: The brain is a wonderful thing.
Sam: Why do you say that?
Bobby: Because it starts working the second you get up in the morning and never stops until you get asked a question in class!

Playing truant from school is like a credit card:
Fun now, pay later!

Teacher: Be sure that you go straight home.
Will: I can't, I live round the corner!

Dinner Lady: What's the matter with your lunch?
Pupil: Can you tell me what it is in case I need to tell my doctor later what I've eaten?

Little Cannibal: I hate my teacher.
Mother Cannibal: Well just eat your salad up then, dear!

Mother: Why did you just swallow the money I gave you?
Son: Well you did say it was for my lunch!

What tables don't you have to learn?
Dinner tables!

Teacher: Can anyone tell me what sort of animal a slug is?
Pupil: It's a snail with a housing problem!

What did the zero say to the eight?
Nice belt!

Why did the cyclops stop teaching?
It had only one pupil!

A group of school students were on a field trip to the local police station. Several of the children were fascinated by the "Wanted" posters on the wall. Little Billy raised his hand and asked the policeman giving them the tour who the people on the wall were.
"Those are pictures of criminals we are looking for," answered the policeman. "We call those 'Wanted' posters." Little Billy looked puzzled. His hand went back up into the air.
"Why didn't you just keep hold of them when you took their picture?"

What fur do we get from a tiger?
As fur as possible!

Teacher: Give me three reasons why the world is round.
Pupil: Well my dad says so, my mum says so, and you say so!

Teacher: Are you good at mathematics?
Pupil: Yes and no.
Teacher: What do you mean?
Pupil: Yes, I'm no good at mathematics!

Jason: I got 100% in school today.
Mother: Wonderful. What did you get 100 in?
Jason: Two things: I got 50% in Spelling
and 50% in History!

What kind of pliers do you use in arithmetic?
Multipliers!

Teacher: If you had one pound and you asked your father for another, how many pounds would you have?
Jake: One pound.
Teacher: You don't know your arithmetic.
Jake: You don't know my Dad!

Teacher: Sam, what's an autobiography?
Sam: The story of a car, of course!

Teacher: What shape is the planet we live in?
Pupil: Terrible!

Teacher: When you yawn, you're supposed to put your hand to your mouth!
Pupil: What, and get bitten?!

Mother: What did you learn in school today?
Son: How to write.
Mother: Great! What did you write?
Son: I don't know, they haven't taught us how to read yet!

When I was your age I thought nothing of walking 5 miles to school.
I agree, I don't think much of it myself!

What do we do with crude oil?
Teach it some manners!

My dog is great at mathematics.
Really?
Ask him how much is two minus two...
But two minus two is nothing!
That's what he'll say, nothing!

My Geography Teacher is so Stupid he Thinks...

...the English Channel is on satellite TV

...Ben Nevis has a brother named Bill

...New York is 5 hours behind London because London was discovered first

...the Cheddar Gorge is a big cheese sandwich

...the language in Cuba is cubic

...birds fly South for the winter because they can't afford the train fare

...a volcano is a mountain with hiccups

...Germany is where germs come from

...A fjord is a Norwegian car

...The Rocky Mountains are named after Sylvester Stallone

Dinner Lady: Eat up your greens, they are good for your skin.
Pupil: But I don't want green skin!

I failed every subject except for algebra. How did you keep from failing that?
I didn't take algebra!

Teacher: If 1+1=2 and 2+2=4, what is 4+4?
Pupil: That's not fair! You answered the easy ones and leave us with the hard one!

Finding one of her students making faces at others in the playground, Mrs. Smith stopped to gently correct the girl. Smiling sweetly, the teacher said, "When I was a child, I was told if I made ugly faces I would stay like that." The girl looked up and replied,
"Well you can't say you weren't warned!"

Where is the best place to have the sickroom at school?
Next to the canteen!

How did the dinner lady get an electric shock?
She stepped on a bun and a current went up her leg!

What's a mushroom?
The place they store the school food!

Teacher: Can you count to 10?
Billy: Yes, Miss. One, two, three, four, five, six, seven, eight, nine, ten.
Teacher: Good. Now can you count any higher?
Billy: Sure. Do you want me to stand on a chair?

Teacher: Do you file your nails Billy?
Billy: No, I just throw them away!

Pupil: I thought we got a choice for dinner, but there is only burnt sausages and soggy chips!
Dinner Lady: That's the choice, take it or leave it!

"Darling," said Mrs Beldon, "Tim's teacher says he ought to have an encyclopedia."
"Encyclopedia, my eye!" said Mr Beldon.
"He can walk to school like I had to!"

Teacher: Can you count to 10?
Brooklyn: Yes, Miss. One, two, three, four, five, six, seven, eight, nine, ten.
Teacher: Now go on from there...
Brooklyn: Jack, Queen, King...

Teacher: I told you to stand at the end of the queue.
Pupil: I tried, but there was someone already there!

Why don't you see giraffes in college?
Because they're all in High School!

Teacher: Why does the Statue of Liberty stand in New York harbour?
Pupil: Because it can't sit down!

Pupil: I don't like cheese with holes.
Dinner Lady: Well, just eat the cheese and leave the holes on the side of your plate!

Early one morning, a Mum went in to wake up her son. "Get up, it's time to go to school!" "But why, Mum? I don't want to go!" "Give me two reasons why you don't want to go." "Well, the kids hate me for one, and the teachers hate me, too!" "Oh, that's no reason not to go to school. Come on now and get ready." "Give me two reasons why I should go to school." "Well, for one, you're 52 years old. And for another, you're the Headmaster!"

Teacher: Where was the Queen crowned?
Gary: On her head?

Pupil: I don't think I deserved the 0% you gave me for that test.
Teacher: Neither do I, but it's the lowest I could give!

Teacher: Daniela, would you rather have ten ice creams, or six times three ice creams?
Daniela: Ten.
Teacher: No, six times three is eighteen!
Daniela: I know, I don't like ice cream.

It's important to wear glasses during mathematics because it improves de-vision...

Teacher: Are you chewing gum?
Anthony: No, I'm Anthony Johnstone, Miss!

Teacher: You're talking again, James! Do you think you are the teacher of this class?
James: No, Miss.
Teacher: Then stop behaving like a idiot!

A sixth grade class is doing some spelling drills. The teacher asks Tommy if he can spell 'before'. He stands up and says, "B-E-P-H-O-R."
The teacher says, "No, that's wrong. Can anyone else spell 'before'?" Another little boy stands up and says, "B-E-F-O-O-R." Again the teacher says, "No, that's wrong." The teacher asks, "Jethro, can you spell 'before'?" Jethro stands up and says, "B-E-F-O-R-E." "Excellent Jethro, now can you use it in a sentence?"
Jethro says, "That's easy. Two plus two be fore..."

Teacher: How much is half of 8?
Pupil: Up and down or across?
Teacher: What do you mean?
Pupil: Well, up and down makes a 3 or across the middle leaves a 0!

Pupil: Do hams grow on plants?
Teacher: No, it's a meat.
Pupil: So what's an ambush?

Mother: What courses are you taking again, Penelope?
Penelope: Algebra and French.
Mother: How do you say "Hello" in Algebra?

Teacher: How did they divide the Roman Empire?
Sarah: With a pair of Caesars!

Teacher: If you got £10 from 20 people, what would you have?
Mikey: A Playstation!

Biology Teacher: What do we call the outermost layer of a tree?
Ryan: Don't know, Miss!
Biology Teacher: Bark, you idiot!
Ryan: Woof, woof!

Teacher: I wish you would pay a little attention!
Pupil: I'm paying as little as I can!

Julie: What's that mark on your shoulder, Miss?
Teacher: It's a birth mark, Julie.
Julie: Oh, have you had it long?

A teacher asked one of the boys in her class, "Can people predict the future with cards?" The boy said, "My Mum can." The teacher replied, "Really?"
The boy said, "Yes, she takes one look at my report card and tells me what will happen when my Dad gets home!"

Pupil: Is it true that people from Hong Kong are really thick?
Teacher: Why do you say that?
Pupil: My book says they have the densest population!

Mother: How did you find school today?
Daughter: I just got off the bus and there it was!

Where did the pilgrims land when they came to America?
On their feet!

Why does history keep repeating itself?
Because we weren't listening the first time!

Who succeeded the first President of the USA?
The second one!

What did Noah do while spending time on the Ark?
Fished, but he didn't catch much. He had only two worms!

Did you hear about the kid that was named after his father?
They called him Dad!

What do you do to a troublesome chick?
Eggspell him!

Who invented fractions?
Henry the Eighth!

What was the first thing Queen Elizabeth did on reaching the throne?
She sat down!

Teacher: When was Rome built?
Pupil: At night.
Teacher: Why did you say that?
Pupil: Because my Dad always says that Rome wasn't built in a day!

Why were the early days of history called the dark ages?
Because there were so many knights!

When a knight in armour was killed in battle, what sign did they put on his grave?
Rust in peace!

What was Camelot famous for?
The knight life!

Tony: I got an "A" in spelling, Dad!
Dad: You idiot! There's no "A" in "spelling"!

What did the Sheriff of Nottingham say when Robin fired at him?
That was an arrow escape!

Who can tell me where Hadrian's Wall is?
I expect it's around Hadrian's garden!

Teacher: Why are you picking your nose in class?
Pupil: My mother won't let me do it at home!

Teacher: Does anyone know who broke the sound barrier?
Pupil: I never touched it!

Teacher: How would the world be different if Edison hadn't invented the light bulb?
Bobby: We'd all be playing Nintendo by candlelight!

Aliens Ate My Homework
and some other brilliant excuses...

Some aliens from outer space ate it

I lost it fighting this kid who
said you weren't the best
teacher in the school

My pet gerbil's had babies,
and they used it to make a nest

Some other aliens from outer space
borrowed it so they could study
how the human brain worked

I put it in a safe,
but lost the combination

I left it in my shirt and my mother
put it in the washing machine

I didn't do it because I didn't want to add to your already heavy workload

A sudden gust of wind blew it out of my hand and I never saw it again

Teacher: You seem very well read: have you read Shakespeare?
Pupil: No.
Teacher: What have you read, then?
Pupil: Um... I've red hair!

Mum: "Did you enjoy the school outing?"
Donna: "Yes, and we're going back tomorrow."
Mum: "What for?"
Donna: "To look for the children who got left behind."

Ron: What's the weather whas-name thingy like around Mount Everest, Sir?
Teacher: Climate, Ron.
Ron: "Blimey, I don't want to know that badly!"

Teacher: Jenny, why are you late?
Jenny: There are eight of us in my family and the alarm was only set for seven!

The class was on a field study trip
to the countryside. "That's a nice cow," said
Julia. "That's a Jersey," said the teacher.
"Oh," said Julie, "I thought that was its skin!"

Teacher: If this class doesn't stop making so much noise, I'll go crazy!
Pupil: I think it's too late. We haven't made a sound for an hour!

Pupil: This egg is bad.
Dinner Lady: Don't blame me, I only laid the table!

Teacher: Lee, I hope I didn't see you copying from David's work!
Lee: So do I!

Well, here's my report, Dad.
Well, there is one thing in your favour, son. With grades like this, you can't be cheating!

Teacher: What is the plural of mouse?
Pupil: Mice.
Teacher: Good, now what's the plural of baby?
Pupil: Twins!

Father: You've got 4 F's and a D on your report!
Son: Maybe I concentrated too much on the one subject...

Teacher: Can't you keep anything in your head for longer than five minutes?
Pupil: Of course, I've had this cold in my head for nearly a week!

Teacher: Jane, why do you have such a problem with decimals?
Jane: I just can't see the point, Miss!

"An abstract noun," the teacher said, "is something you can think of, but you can't touch it. Can you give me an example of one?"
"Yes," a teenage boy replied.
"My Dad's new car."

Teacher: You're new here aren't you?
What's your name?
Pupil: Dicky Mickey Smith.
Teacher: I'll call you Dicky Smith then.
Pupil: My dad won't like that.
Teacher: Why is that?
Pupil: He doesn't like people taking the
Mickey out of my name!

Joanne was looking miserable.
She says to her teacher,
"I hate school! I can't believe I have to
stay here until I'm sixteen!"
"I know the feeling," said the teacher,
"I have to stay here till I'm sixty-five..."

Teacher: Johnny, give me a
sentence starting with "I".
Elisa: I is...
Teacher: No, Elisa. Always say, "I am."
Elisa: All right. "I am the ninth letter
of the alphabet."

Teacher: What are you doing, hopping into school ten minutes late?
Pupil: Well, you told me never to stroll into school ten minutes late!

Teacher: "If I cut a potato in two, then in two again, then once more, what do I have?"
Jack: "Chips!"

Teacher: What's the difference between an African and an Indian elephant?
Theresa: About three thousand miles!

What did the French book say to the Maths book?
Let me 'elp you wiz your problems!

George: Look, I just found a lost football.
Louis: How do you know it's lost?
George: Because the kids down the street are still looking for it!

Teacher: I see you've got your Easter shirt on, Martin.
Martin: Why do you call it that, Miss?
Teacher: Because it's got egg on it.

A lady began a job as a school counsellor, and she was eager to help. One day during break she noticed a boy standing by himself on the side of a playing field while the rest of the kids enjoyed a game of football. She approached and asked if he was alright.

The boy said he was fine, thank you.

A little while later, however, she noticed the boy was in the same spot, still by himself. Approaching again, the lady said, "Would you like me to be your friend?" The boy hesitated, then said, "OK," looking at the woman suspiciously. Feeling she was making progress, she then asked, "Why are you standing here all alone? Why don't you go and join those boys playing football over there?"

"Because," the little boy said, "I'm the goalkeeper."

Teacher: Don't you cut your hair any longer?
Fred: No, sir, I cut it shorter!

Sarah: Why were you late for school?
Jan: I had to say goodbye to my pets.
Sarah: But you were 2 hours late!
Jan: I have an ant farm!

Teacher: Charles, please use "discount"
in a sentence.
Charles: Yes, ma'am.
Does discount as a sentence?

Pupils: Can we go outside and watch the
solar eclipse?
Teacher: All right, but don't stand too close!

Danny: I can't solve this problem.
Teacher: What? Any five-year-old should
be able to solve this one!
Danny: No wonder I can't do it then,
I'm nearly ten!

Teacher: What's a wombat?
Frank: Something you play Wom with?

Can you tell me where elephants are found?

You don't have to find elephants, they're so big, they never get lost!

A policeman sees a small boy in a pub drinking a pint of beer and smoking. "Hey! Why aren't you at school?" he says.
"I don't have to go to school," says the kid, "I'm only four."

Teacher: Didn't you promise to behave?
Sean: Yes, sir.
Teacher: And didn't I promise to punish you if you didn't?
Sean: Yes, sir, but since I broke my promise, you didn't have to keep yours!

What is the difference between a school teacher and a train?
The teacher says 'Spit your gum out' and the train says 'chew chew chew'!

Teacher: Frank, if you had £8 in one pocket and £11 in the other, what would you have?
Frank: Someone else's trousers on!

Biology Teacher: Why do whales have waterproof skin?
Pupil: To keep their insides from falling out!

Dad, we're collecting for the new swimming pool at school.
Hang on, I'll get you a glass of water!

Cookery Teacher: Fred, there were two chocolate cakes in the stock room before break, and now there's only one. Why?
Fred: I don't know. It must have been so dark I didn't see the other one!

Do you think there should be a club for kids who like Maths?
No, you don't have to beat them, just ignore them!

Teacher: What's the capital of France, Jenny?
Jenny: F?

Teacher: Sean, if you had £2, and eggs were a 50p a dozen, how many would you buy?
Sean: "None, Miss."
Teacher: "None?"
Sean: "No, if I had £2, I'd get a Big Mac and fries!"

Billy: I failed everything except biology.
Mum: How did you keep from failing that?
Billy: I overslept!

Teacher: What did the pencil say to the rubber?
Jim: Take me to your ruler!

In what school do you learn how to greet people?
Hi school!

Teacher: Say, you can't sleep in my class.
Student: I could if you didn't talk so loud!

Dinner Lady: It's very rude to reach over the table for the salt, haven't you got a tongue in your head?

Pupil: Yes, but my arms are longer!

Billy phones his Mum one day. "Mum, I fell off the bike shed roof today and broke four ribs." "Gracious!" says his Mum. "Which hospital did they take you to?" "I didn't go to hospital," says Billy. "What? You've got four broken ribs and they didn't take you to hospital?" his Mum screams. "Oh they weren't my ribs," says Billy, "I landed on Sally Jameson!"

Tony is having an eye test at school. "Can you read the top line of letters on the chart, Tony?" said the nurse. "No," said Tony. "How about the second line, can you read that?" said the nurse. "Nope," said Tony. "Can you read the bottom line, then?" said the nurse. "No," said Tony, "I can't read at all, yet."

Teacher: Matthew, what is the climate like in New Zealand?

Matthew: Really, really cold.

Teacher: It's not that cold, actually.

Matthew: You're joking, when they send us lamb, it's frozen solid!

Teacher: What noise does a squirrel make?

Kelly: Woof Woof?

Teacher: Squirrels don't go "Woof Woof"!

Kelly: It says in this book that squirrels eat acorns and bark!

Teacher: Sara, if you had 16 chocolates, and Vernon asked you for 10, how many would you have left?

Sara: Sixteen. I hate Vernon.

Teacher: Dean, if I say "I have went," is that right or wrong?

Dean: Wrong. You ain't gone nowhere. You're still 'ere innit?

Teacher: Did you parents help you with these homework problems?
Pupil: No I got them wrong all by myself!

Why did the pioneers cross the country in covered wagons?
Because they didn't want to wait 40 years for a train!

Teacher: Can anyone tell me how many seconds there are in a year?
Pupil: Twelve, Miss - 2nd January, 2nd February, 2nd March...!

Teacher: Simon. Give me a sentence with the words defence, defeat and detail in it.
Simon: When a horse jumps over defence, defeat go before detail!

Teacher: What can we do to stop polluting our waters?
Pupil: Stop taking baths?

What kind of lighting did Noah use for the Ark?
Floodlights!

Little Johnny was having problems in school. He was always bringing home bad grades and was especially bad in reading. When receiving his report card one day he got all excited and ran home to show his father. He handed his father the report card and proudly says, "Look dad, I got a 'B' in Reading." His dad looks at the report card and gets furious. He looks down at Johnny and says, "You idiot, that's a 'D'!"

Teacher: You aren't paying attention to me. Are you having trouble hearing?
Pupil: No, I'm having trouble listening!

Teacher: Spell "Aardvark".
Student: I don't know how.
Teacher: Well, look it up in the dictionary!
Student: How can I look up a word to spell in the dictionary if I don't know how to spell the word in the first place?

Why did the teacher put the lights on?
Because the class was so dim!

Teacher: Now class, whatever I ask, I want you to all answer at once. How much is 6 plus 4?

Class: At once!

Teacher: What's happens to gold when it is exposed to the air?

Barry: Someone nicks it!

Teacher: Nicky? Didn't you hear me call you?

Nicky: Yes, but you told us not to answer back!

Teacher: Billy, please don't whistle while you're working.

Billy: Oh, I'm not working - just whistling!

Teacher: If I had ten flies on my desk and I swatted one, how many would be left?

Pupil: One - the others would have flown off!

Teacher: What does the 1286BC written on the mummy's tomb indicate?
Student: The registration of the car that ran him over!

Teacher: Does anyone know which month has 28 days?
Gary: All of them!

Sally was hungry, so she went into a baker's shop. "How much are a couple of buns?" she said. "Two for 25p," said the shopkeeper. "How much for one?" Sally asked. "One is 13p," said the shopkeeper.
Sally thought for a second.
"I'll take the other one!"

Teacher: What's your name?
Pupil: Jason.
Teacher: You should say "Sir".
Pupil: OK, Sir Jason!

Barney: My grandad was a hunter in Scotland. He used to go hunting lions! Kev: You liar! There aren't any lions in Scotland!

Barney: There aren't any now — my grandad shot them all!

Why do teachers use a bamboo cane?

Because when the cane goes "bam" the child goes "boo"!

Teacher: William, please use the word "window" in a sentence.

William: OK. I entered a competition, but I didn't "window!"

Teacher: Simon, can you give me a good example of how heat expands things and cold contracts them?

Simon: Well, I've noticed that the days tend to be longer in the summer and shorter in the winter!

How do you know carrots are good for your eyesight?

Did you ever see a rabbit wearing glasses?

Teacher: What is a comet?
Pupil: A star with a tail.
Teacher: Can you name one?
Pupil: Mickey Mouse?

Teacher: Where does your mother come from?
Pupil: Alaska!
Teacher: Don't worry, I'll ask her myself!

Teacher: What is the most common phrase used in school?
Pupil: Dunno, Miss.
Teacher: Correct!

Pupil: What's for lunch today, Rose?
Dinner Lady: The specials today are shepherd's pie and apple crumble.
Pupil: I see... Which one is this?

Teacher: What's a Grecian Urn?
Kate: About 50 Drachmas a week!

Woodwork teacher: You're just like lightning with that hammer, Tony.
Tony: Because I'm so quick, sir?
Woodwork teacher: No, because you never strike in the same place twice!

Teacher: Why do mermaids wear seashells?
Sarah: Because B shells are too small and D shells are too big!

Teacher: What's the difference between roast beef and pea soup?
Danny: Anyone can roast beef, Miss!

Billy: The new Geography teacher's got a wig made out of cat fur!
Emma: Really? How do you know?
Billy: Because every time he scratches his head, his bottom shoots up in the air!

Teacher: Why shouldn't you eat uranium?
Pupil: Because you'll get atomic ache!

Teacher: Fred, I'm glad to see your writing has improved.
Fred: Thank you.
Teacher: Unfortunately, now I can see how bad your spelling is!

Pupil: The art teacher doesn't like what I'm making...
Dad: Why is that? What are you making?
Pupil: A mess!

Teacher: Which one burns longer, a black one or a white one?
Pupil: Neither, they both burn shorter!

Teacher: Belinda. Can you find me Australia on the map please?
Belinda: There it is.
Teacher: Well done! Louise, who discovered Australia?
Louise: Belinda did!

Why did Robin Hood rob only the rich?

Because the poor didn't
have anything
worth stealing!

Teacher: Do you want to borrow a pocket calculator?
Pupil: No thanks, I know how many pockets I've got!

Teacher: Karen, stop your day dreaming!
Karen: I wasn't day dreaming, I was taking a nap!

Teacher: What is "can't" short for?
Pupil: Cannot?
Teacher: Right! And what is "don't" short for?
Pupil: Doughnut?

Art Teacher: Michele, what colour are you going to paint the sun and the wind?
Michele: The sun rose, and the wind blue!

Teacher: OK, Bill. In this exam you will be allowed 30 minutes for each question.
Bill: How long do we get for the answers?

Teacher: What is further away, Australia or the Moon?
Pupil: Australia, because you can see the Moon at night!

Tom had this problem of getting up late in the morning and was always late for school. His teacher was angry with him and threatened to expel him if he didn't do something about it. So Tom went to a doctor who gave him a pill and told him to take it before he went to bed to help him sleep. Tom slept well and in fact beat the alarm in the morning. He had breakfast and got the bus to school. He said to the teacher: "I made it, and I slept really well and I feel great!"
"That's all fine," said the teacher, "But where were you yesterday?"

Teacher: Do we all know what adding is?
Susie: It's the noise my doorbell makes!

Teacher: Mark, I told you to write this poem out 10 times to improve your handwriting and you've only done it 7 times...
Mark: That's because my maths is rubbish as well!

Teacher: This is the third time I've had to tell you off this week: what have you got to say about that?
Pupil: I'm glad it's Friday!

Teacher: Why can't you ever answer any of my questions?
Pupil: Well if I could, there wouldn't be much point in my being here!

Teacher: Why weren't you in school yesterday?
Damien: I was sick.
Teacher: Sick of what?
Damien: Sick of school!

Troy: Mum, I got sent home because the boy next to me in class was smoking!

Mum: The boy next to you? Why didn't they send him home, then?

Troy: Cos it was me that set him on fire!

Donny: How do I measure this ladder?
Teacher: Lay it on the ground
and pace it out.
Donny: But I want to know
how tall it is, not how long!

Teacher: Samantha, you copied these
answers from Monica, didn't you?
Samantha: What makes you say that?
Teacher: Because her answer to question 5
is "I don't know," and yours is "Me neither".

Biology Teacher: Barney, what do you get
hanging from Horse Chestnut trees?
Barney: Sore arms!

Teacher: Good grief, Darren. R-O-X
doesn't spell rocks!
Darren: Really? What does it spell then?

Teacher : Were you copying his sums?
Pupil : No! Just seeing if he got mine right!

"What's your father's occupation?"
asked the school secretary on the
first day of the new school year.
"He's a magician, Miss," said the new boy.
"How interesting. What's his favourite trick?"
"He saws people in half."
"Gosh! Now, next question: do you have any
brothers or sisters?"
"Yes, one half brother and two half sisters."

Teacher: How many bones do we
have in our body?
Harry: I have a couple of
thousand, I should think.
Teacher: How do you make that out?
Harry: I had sardines for lunch!

Which Queen was the longest on the throne?
The one that was the tallest standing up!

Teacher 1: My, hasn't Emma Jones grown?
Teacher 2: Yes, she's certainly gruesome!

Teacher: Where were you yesterday, Daisy?
Daisy: At the dentist, Miss. I had a bad tooth.
Teacher: Oh, I'm sorry to hear that. Is it better today?
Daisy: I don't know Miss, the dentist kept it!

Teacher: Sam, why are you spinning on your head?
Sam: I like to do a good turn every day!

Do you know a teacher with one eye called Mr Hargreaves?
No, what's his other eye called?

Headmaster: Smith, come here! I'll teach you to throw stones at the school minibus!
Smith: I wish you would, Sir. I keep missing it!

What kind of food do maths teachers eat?
Square meals!

Biology Teacher: What's an indication of iron deficiency?
Fiona: Wrinkly clothes, Miss!

Why was 6 afraid of 7?
Because 789!

Jerry: I'm worried about the exams, Miss. I bumped my head and now I can't remember anything!
Teacher: When did this happen?
Jerry: When did what happen?

Why is Alabama the cleverest state in the USA?
Because it has 4 A's and one B!

Teacher: Where is the English Channel?
Sid: I don't know, we haven't got cable!

What do you measure farm vehicles with?
A protractor!

Teacher: What came after the stone age and the bronze age?
Pupil: The sausage?

**What do Mallards keep their
schoolbooks in?**
A ducksack!

**Why does the school brass band
march while they play?**
They're trying to get away from the noise!

**Geography Teacher: How many balls of
string would it take to reach the moon?**
Pupil: Just one if it's long enough!

**Arthur: There is definitely a connection
between television and violence.
Martha: What makes you think that?**
Arthur: Because I told my Mum I had
watched television instead of doing my
homework, and she hit me!

**Teacher: Did you sister help you with
your homework, David?**
David: No, she did it all!

Physics Teacher: Tim, who might use microwaves?
Tim: Very small surfers?

Where do children learn their ABC's?
At LMN-tary school!

What do ghosts write their homework in?
Exorcise books!

Science Teacher: What is the centre of gravity?
Pupil: The letter V!

English Teacher: Which is the longest word you can think of?
Pupil: "Smiles", because there is a mile between each "s"!

Why did the Tyrannosaurus stand in the corner?
Because he'd been naughty!

My History Teacher is so stupid, he thinks...

...Joan of Arc was Noah's wife!

... and Noah was an Ark-itect!

...That "Gladiator" was how a cannibal felt after lunch!

... That the Romans built straight roads so their soldiers didn't go around the bend!

... That a Roman forum is two-um plus two-um!

... That a saxophone was a Saxon telephone!

... That King Arthur's round table was made by Sir Circumference!

... That the Vikings send secret messages by Norse code!

... That King Alfred the Grate invented the fireplace!

... That the Black Prince was the son of Old King Cole!

Biology Teacher: Bobby, can you give me an example of a Fungi?
Pupil: Someone with a Playstation who knows lots of dirty jokes?

A small boy went up to a teacher in the playground on his first day of school. "I've lost my brother!" he said. The teacher said, "Don't worry, we'll find him. What's he like?"
The little boy replied, "Crisps and Lego!"

Teacher: What a glum face, what would you say if I came to school with a face like yours?
Pupil: I'd be too polite to mention it!

Maths Teacher: What do you get when you divide the diameter of a pumpkin by its circumference?
Pupil: Pumpkin Pi!

Father: Why did you get such a low score in that maths test?
Son: Absence.
Father: What, you were absent on the day of the maths test?
Son: No but the boy who usually sits next to me was!

I wish I had been born 1,000 years ago. Why is that?
Just think of all the history that I wouldn't have to learn!

A boy comes into class with a carrot up his nose and a sausage in each ear. "I'm not feeling very well, Miss," he says. "I'm not surprised," says the teacher.
"You obviously aren't eating properly!"

Mother: Let me see your report, son.
Son: Here it is, Mum, but don't show it to Dad. He's been helping me!

Chemistry Teacher: What is copper nitrate?
Pupil: Overtime for policemen!

A teacher catches an older girl in school whom she doesn't recognise. "Who are you, young lady?" she says. "Maddy Jones, Miss," says the girl. "I don't know you, can you identify yourself?" says the teacher. The girl gets a mirror out of her bag and looks into it...
"Yes," she says, "that's definitely me!"

Geography Teacher: What would happen if the Thames Flood Barrier broke?
Pupil: It would be a dam shame, sir!

Why should fish be clever?
Because they hang around in schools!

What do small music students sit at?
Compact Desks!

"Sara, can you name two living things that don't have any teeth?" asked the science teacher.

Sara: "Yes. Granny and Grandpa."

Mr Hubbins, the deputy headmaster, needed to use a pay phone, but didn't have change for a pound. He saw Billy Wiggins in the corridor, and asked him, "Wiggins, do you have change for a pound coin?"
Billy shrugged and replied, "Yes, Mate."
Mr Hubbins turned red.
"Wiggins, that's no way to address a teacher! What's the matter with you? Are you worthless AND stupid? Now let's try it again... Wiggins, do you have change for a pound coin?"
Billy replied, "No, SIR!"

Why wasn't Cinderella picked for the school hockey team?
She kept running away from the ball!

And why did Cinderella never get good at netball?
Because her coach was a pumpkin!

A school party to the Natural History Museum are looking at the dinosaur bones. One of the students asks the guard, "Can you tell me how old the dinosaur bones are?" The guard replies, "They are 3 million, four years, and six months old." "Wow!" says the student, "How do you know their age so exactly?" The guard answers, "Well, the dinosaur bones were three million years old when I started working here, and that was four and a half years ago."

Donald: Sorry I'm late, my canary died of flu. Teacher: I didn't know canaries could die of flu... Donald: Mine did, it flew into a bus!

Bobby was a very clever little boy. Whenever he got an 'A' at school, his Dad would give him ten pence and a pat on the head. By the time he was sixteen he had two hundred pounds and a flat head!

Wrong! Some definitely daft definitions:

Abundance - A baker's disco

Arcade - A lemonade-type drink served on Noah's Ark

Avoidable - What a bullfighter tries to do

Contents - Where con men sleep while camping

Cowhide - Game played by cows

Eclipse - What a barber does for a living

Eyedropper - A clumsy ophthalmologist

Fan Club - A weapon used by a celebrity

Fire Escape - A way for a fire to go out

Handicap - A hat cover that is easy to find and wear

Hardship - A ship protected by tough cover

Hatchet - What a hen does to an egg

Hence - An enclosure around a hen yard

Heroes - What a guy in a boat does

Himalaya - A rooster that makes an egg

Holy Smoke - The church is on fire

Illegal - A sick bird
Life Jacket - A special long-lasting coat
Matchbook - A book about matches
Misty - How golfers create divots

Cowhide

Wrong! More definitely daft definitions:

Mohair - What bald-headed men need
Network - The process of making nets
Paradox - Two Doctors
Pharmacist - A helper on the farm
Piggyback - A lost pig is back home
Polarise - What penguins see with
Polite - A light on a pole
Polygon - A parrot that got away
Protest - Testing a professional person
Relief - What trees do in the spring
Remind - A brain transplant
Showoff - The show has been cancelled
Selfish - What the owner of a
fish shop does
Subdued - A dude who works on
a submarine
Weekend - A book with a rubbish ending
Whether - Unpredictable weather
Writer - One who corrects a wrong

PART THREE
DISGUSTING JOKES

Mummy! I keep running in circles.
Shut up or I'll nail your other foot to the floor!

The first time Esmerelda met the Hunchback of Notre Dame she was shopping with her friend; she saw the hideous hunchback and was aghast - she had to speak to him... "Goodness! How did you get so ugly?" she said. Quasimodo replied: "Well, when I was younger and I couldn't reach the bell rope, I'd climb up to the belfry and ring the bell by bashing my head against it." "I see!" said Esmerelda, and she went back to her friend. "Who was that?" her friend asked.
"I don't know," said Esmerelda.
"But his face rings a bell..."

When do cannibals leave the table?
When everyone's eaten!

What do you call a cow with no legs?
Ground Beef!

There was a farmer who grew watermelons. He was doing pretty well, but he was plagued by local children who would sneak into his patch at night and steal his watermelons. After some careful thought he comes up with a brilliantly clever idea that he thinks will scare the kids away for sure. So he makes up a sign and sticks it in the field. The sign says, "Warning, one of the watermelons in this field has been poisoned." The farmer goes to inspect his field the next morning and finds a new sign that says:

"Warning, now two of the watermelons in this field have been poisoned."

Where does an Eskimo pig live?
In a Pigloo!

Why was the sand wet?
Because the sea-weed!

A three-legged dog walks into a saloon in the Old West.
He sidles up to the bar and announces:
"I'm looking for the man who shot my paw!"

A man goes to the doctor with a problem. "You have to help me, Doc. I think I'm a kleptomaniac: I can't stop myself stealing things!" "Take these pills," says the Doctor. "They might help." "But what if they don't?" says the man. "See if you can get me a DVD player, will you?"

Mummy! What happens to all that dog food Patch doesn't eat? Shut up and eat your meatloaf!

What do you call a bad lion tamer? Claude Bottom!

Cannibal husband: What's for lunch, Dear? Cannibal Wife: Salad. Cannibal Husband: Can't we open a tin of someone?

One day a pirate and a bartender were talking to each other in a pub. The bartender asked the pirate, "Where did you get that wooden leg from?" "Arr," the pirate said, "we were sailing the seven seas when a big old shark came up to me while I was swimmin' and bit off me leg."

The bartender then asked, "And how did you get that hook?" "Arr," the pirate said, "me crew and I were in a mighty battle and it got cut through the bone wi' a cutlass." The bartender then asked, "Then where did ya get the eye patch from?" The pirate said, "In a harbour I looked at a gull flying overhead and it took a dump right in me eye." The bartender was puzzled and asked the pirate, "How would that make you get an eye patch?"

The pirate looked sad. "Arr," he said, "twas me first day with me new hook."

What has four legs and an arm?
A happy Rottweiler!

"My girlfriend is one of identical twins."
"Really? How do you tell them apart?"
"Her brother's got a beard."

What is the last thing to go through a
bug's mind before
he hits the windscreen?
His bum!

How do you keep flies out of
the kitchen?
Put a big pile of manure in the living room!

A stone-age hunter walking through the
jungle found a huge dead dinosaur with a
little pygmy standing beside it. Amazed,
he asked: "Did you kill that?"
The pygmy said, "Yes."
The hunter asked, "How could a little
bloke like you kill a huge dinosaur like
that?" The pygmy said:
"I killed it with my club."

The astonished hunter asked:
"How big is your club?"
The pygmy replied: "There's about 60 of us."

Teacher: Where was Joan of Arc burned?
Dan: All over her body!

Two cannibals sat beside a large fire, after eating the best meal they'd had in ages. "Your wife sure makes a good roast," said the first cannibal.
"Yeah," replied the second, "I'm really going to miss her..."

What do you call a dog with no legs?
Doesn't matter... he won't come to you anyway!

Why didn't the skeleton go to the party?
He had no body to go with!

What happened to the kid who drank eight Cokes?
He burped Seven-up!

How can you tell if a corpse is angry?
It flips its lid!

Waiter, I've got a maggot in my salad!
Well, it's better than half a maggot!

How can you tell which end is which on a worm?
Put it in a bowl of flour and wait till it farts!

What happened at the cannibal's wedding party?
They toasted the bride and groom!

Superman bumped into the Incredible Hulk. "Are you still seeing that girl Helen?" he said. "Nah, she bled to death from the flu," the Hulk said. Superman said, "You don't bleed to death from the flu!"
The Hulk said, "You do if you give it to me!"

The best cannibal's cookbook is called 'How to Better Serve your Fellow Man'.
It was written by a man who had a wife and ate kids!

I have five eyes, three green ears and
a yellow nose, what am I?
Really ugly!

What is the height of stupidity?
I don't know, how tall are you?

Three missionaries in Africa
were captured by a tribe of very hostile
cannibals who put them in a large pot of
water, built a huge fire under it, and left
them there. A few minutes later, one of
the missionaries started to laugh
uncontrollably. The other missionaries
were appalled, and one said,
"What's wrong with you? We're being
boiled alive! They're going to eat us!
What could possibly be funny
at a time like this?"
The laughing missionary said,
"I just weed in the soup!"

The Dead Dog

A man runs into a vet's office carrying his dog, screaming for help. The vet has him put his dog down on the table. The vet examines the still, limp body and tells the man that his dog, unfortunately, is dead. The man, clearly upset, demands a second opinion. The vet goes into the back room and brings in a black labrador. The lab sniffs the body, walks from head to tail, and finally looks at the vet and barks. The vet looks at the man and says, "I'm sorry, but the labrador thinks your dog is dead too." The man, finally accepting the diagnosis, thanks the vet and asks how much he owes. The vet answers, "£650." "£650 to tell me my dog is dead?" exclaimed the man. "Well," the vet replies, "I would have charged you only £50 for my initial diagnosis. The additional £600 was for the lab tests."

"I've got a chicken that lays square eggs," said the farmer.

"Really, that's amazing," his friend said.

"Yep, and not only that, it talks as well!" said the farmer.

"No! What does it say?" said his mate.

"It says 'OUCH!'"

Did you hear the joke about the fart?

You don't want to, it stinks!

What do cannibals eat on toast?

Baked Beings!

"Doctor, my tummy hurts! I've just eaten four red snooker balls, two blue snooker balls and a pink snooker ball."

"No wonder you're not feeling well, you aren't eating enough greens!"

Did you hear about the Indian chief who drank 15 cups of tea before bed-time?
That night he drowned in his tea-pee!

Why does the boy monster kiss the girl monster on the back of her neck?
That's where her lips are!

Why did the toilet paper roll down the hill?
Because it wanted to get to the bottom!

What's disgusting and visits Earth once every 80 years?
Halley's Vomit!

An Apache is lying in the road with his ear to the ground when a cowboy comes by. The Apache says, "Stagecoach went by here half an hour ago."

**The cowboy says,
"Wow, how do you know that?"**
The Apache says, "Broke my damn neck."

**Why did the chewing gum
cross the road?**
It was stuck to the leg of a chicken!

What do you call a man with no legs?
Neil!

**What do you get when you toss a hand
grenade into a French kitchen?**
Linoleum blownapart!

Why did the monkey fall out of the tree?
Because it was dead!

**Why did the bald man put rabbits
on his head?**
Someone said that from a distance they
looked like hares!

**What do you call a man with cow
droppings all over his feet?**
An incowpoop!

A man wakes up from an operation and the doctor tells him,
"I've got good news and bad news for you."
So the man says,
"OK, give me the bad news first."
And the doctor says,
"We've made a mistake and cut off the wrong leg." After a while the man pulls himself together and says,
"So what's the good news?"
and the doctor replies,
"We ran a second check and decided we didn't need to cut your leg off at all!"

Why did the zombie fail his driving test?
He left his foot on the clutch!

Why did Henry VIII have so many wives?
He liked to chop and change!

What do vegetarian cannibals eat?
Swedes!

Two flies are sitting on a dog doodoo,
and one of them burps...
"Do you mind?" says one,
"I'm trying to eat here!"

**What's red, has wheels and lies
on its back?**
A dead bus!

Who looks after sick dwarves?
The national elf service!

Tim was in the garden filling a hole
when his neighbour peered over the
fence. Interested in what the cheeky-
faced youngster was up to, he politely
asked, 'What are you up to there, Tim?'
'My goldfish died,' replied Tim tearfully,
without looking up, 'and I've just buried
him.' The neighbour said,
'That's an awfully big hole for a
goldfish isn't it, Tim?'

**Tim patted down the last heap of earth,
and then replied,**

'That's because he's still inside your
stupid cat.'

A man goes to the optician to have his glass eye cleaned. The optician says, "I can't do it now, but leave it with me and I'll deliver it to you this afternoon. Where do you live?"
"Just round the corner, in Station Road," **says the man. "Righto, I'll be round about 4 o'clock," says the optician.**
"Great," says the man.
"I'll keep an eye out for you!"

Mummy! When are we going to have Aunt Edna for dinner?
Shut up, we haven't even finished Gran yet!

A man and his friend were travelling on a train and they decided to eat a banana. Just as the first man took a bite of his, the train entered a tunnel and everything went dark. The man said to his friend:
"Don't eat your banana!
I took one bite and I went blind!"

What's a skeleton?
Bones with the person off!

This man decides to start up a chicken farm, so he buys a hundred chickens to get up and running. A month later he returns to the dealer to get another hundred chickens because the first lot had died. Another month passes and he's back at the dealers for another hundred chickens, "I don't know what's wrong," he tells the dealer,
"Do you think I'm planting them too deep?"

Did you hear about the lumberjack that lost his left arm and leg in a chainsaw accident?
He's all right now!

Did you hear about the cannibal's daughter?
She was ate before she was seven!

How do you make a shepherd's pie?
First peel two shepherds...

A woman walked up to a little old man rocking in a chair on his porch. "I couldn't help noticing how happy you look," she said. "What's your secret for a long happy life?" "I smoke three packs of cigarettes a day," he said, "I also drink a case of whisky a week, eat fatty foods, and never exercise!"
"That's amazing," the woman said, "how old are you?'
He thought for a moment, and replied, "Twenty-six."

Why are monsters huge and hairy and ugly?
Because if they were small and round and smooth they'd be M&M's!

How about the bear that was hit by an 18-wheeler and splattered all over the place?
They said it was a grizzly accident.

What do you get if you cross a Rottweiler with a Saint Bernard?
A dog that bites your arm off and goes for help!

What is a polygon?
A dead parrot!

How do you know that owls are cleverer than chickens?
Have you ever heard of Kentucky-fried owl?

What goes "Ha, ha, ha, plop"?
A man laughing his head off!

A man goes to the doctor with terrible wind. "It's funny, Doc. I pass wind every two minutes, but it has no smell and makes no noise." The Doctor gives him some pills and the next day the man is back. "Doc, I'm still passing wind, and they still make no noise, but now they smell awful!" The Doctor says,
"Good, we've cured your blocked nose, now let's do something about your hearing!"

A teacher was asking her class what their grandfathers did. When she asked young Johnny, he said, "My grandfather's dead, Miss." "Oh, I am sorry, Johnny. In that case, what did he do before he died?" "He went blue and fell over, Miss."

Barber: Sir, were you wearing a red scarf when you came in? Customer: No... Barber: Oh dear, I think I've cut your throat!

Dentist: Good grief! You've got the biggest cavity I've ever seen! The biggest cavity I've ever seen! Patient: You don't have to say it twice. Dentist: I didn't, that was an echo!

What do you call a man with no arms and legs in a swimming pool? Bob!

Your Dad is so Stupid...

When your Mum said it was chilly outside, he ran outside with a spoon!

He could trip over a cordless phone!

He sold his car for petrol money!

He bought a solar-powered torch!

He took a ruler to bed to see how long he slept!

When he went to take the 44 bus, he took the 22 twice instead!

He jumped out the window and went up!

He sent me a fax with a stamp on it!

Continued...

I told him Christmas was just round the corner and he went looking for it!

If brains were dynamite, he wouldn't have enough to blow his nose!

He went to the airport and saw a sign saying "Airport Left," so he turned around and went home!

He got fired from the M&M factory for throwing away all the W's!

He ordered a cheeseburger from McDonalds and said, "Hold the cheese!"

When he worked at McDonalds and someone ordered small fries, he said, "Hey Boss, all the small ones have gone!"

He tried to throw a bird off a cliff!

He couldn't tell which way a lift was going if I gave him two guesses!

At the bottom of a form where it says Sign Here - He put "Scorpio!"

He sits on the TV, and watches the sofa!

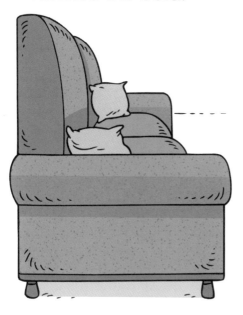

What's the difference between Mozart and a dead body?
One composes, the other decomposes!

Do you think there should be a club for kids who like Robbie Williams?
No, you don't have to beat them, just ignore them!

What do Dutch pet shop owners have on toast?
Hamster jam!

How do you make a Maltese Cross?
Poke him with a stick!

How many pigs does it take to really smell?
A phew!

Cannibal 1: I'm on a diet.
Cannibal 2: Alright, just have a pygmy!

Two Old Ladies

Two old ladies, Millie and Pam, were out driving and they came to some traffic lights. The lights were red but they just went on through. Millie thought to herself, "I could have sworn Pam just drove us through a red light." After a few more minutes they came to another set of lights. The light was red again, and again they went straight through. This time Millie was almost sure that the light had been red... She was getting nervous and decided to pay very close attention to the road and the next set of lights to see what was going on. At the next junction, sure enough, the light was definitely red and they went right through. She turned to Pam and said, "Pam! Did you know we just went through three red lights in a row! You could have killed us!"

Pam turned to her and said,
"Oh, am I driving?"

The Three-Legged Mule

What do you call a mule with three legs?
A wonky donkey!

What do you call a short mule with three legs?
A dinky wonky donkey!

What do you call a short mule with three legs and one eye?
A winky dinky wonky donkey!

What do you call a short mule with three legs and one eye breaking wind?
A stinky winky dinky wonky donkey!

What do you call a short mule with three legs and one eye breaking wind and playing the piano ?
A plinky plonky stinky winky dinky wonky donkey!

What do you call a short mule with three legs and one eye, breaking wind, playing the piano and driving a tractor?

Very clever!

Harry was trying to smuggle a skunk out of America to sell it abroad. He asks his friend the best way to do it. "Just stick it down your trousers," his friend said. "He won't bite unless you sit on him." "But what about the terrible smell?" said Harry. His friend thought for a moment...
"If he dies, he dies!"

Why do cyclists wear lycra shorts?
Because if they didn't, they'd be arrested!

Why shouldn't you put a cat in the washing machine?
In case you get a sock in the puss!

Why do strawberries cry?
Because their mum is in a jam!

What did the monkey say when he cut off his tail?
It won't be long now!

Mummy! Are you sure this is the way to make gingerbread men?
Shut up and get back in the oven!

What's the difference between roast beef and pea soup?
Anyone can roast beef!

Where do you find a no-legged dog?
Wherever you left him.

An artist asked the gallery owner if there had been any interest in his paintings on display at that time. "I have good news and bad news," the owner replied. "The good news is that a man asked about your work and wondered if it would be worth more after your death. I said it would, and he bought all 15 of your paintings."
"That's brilliant!" the artist said.
"What's the bad news?"
"He was your doctor."

Mummy! Why do I have to hop everywhere?
Shut up or I'll chop the other leg off!

A man in the cinema left his seat to go and buy an ice cream. When he came back, he asked an old lady sitting on the aisle. "Excuse me, but did I step on your foot and elbow you in the nose just now?"
"Yes, you did!" said the lady indignantly.
"Oh good," said the man, "this is my row then."

Is it good manners to eat fried chicken with your fingers?
No, you should eat your fingers separately!

What is pig swill?
It's what pigs write before they die so their piglets can have their money!

Did you hear about the man that got the sack from the zoo for feeding the penguins?

He fed them to the tigers!

A man goes to see his doctor feeling a bit unwell. The doctor checks him over and eventually finds a couple of bags of money stuck up his bottom. He pulls them out and can't resist totalling up the value of the coins. "Well," says the doctor, "I've found £1,999 up your bottom."
"Hmmm," replies the patient, "that would explain why I haven't been feeling too grand!"

What happened when the ghost asked for a whisky at his local bar?
The bartender said, "Sorry sir, we don't serve spirits here!"

Why did the cannibal live on his own?
He was fed up with other people!

What does a vampire fear most?
Tooth decay!

Two hunters, not the sharpest tools in the box, went duck hunting one morning with their dogs. After four hours with no success, Bobby says,
"I know what we're doing wrong, Terry: We're not throwing the dogs high enough..."

What's pink and grey and wrinkly and old and belongs to Grandpa monster?
Grandma monster!

What do you get when you cross Bambi with a ghost?
Bamboo!

What's small and cuddly and bright purple?
A koala holding his breath!

Did you hear about the cannibal who loved fast food?
He ordered a pizza with everybody on it!

A woman went to see a psychiatrist and complained, "Doctor, my husband thinks he's a magician." "What's so bad about that?" the Doctor asked. "We're being sued. A week ago my husband shoved a girl into a trunk and sawed it in half."
"The girl's family is suing you?" the psychiatrist asked.
"No, the circus," the woman replied. "The elephant bled to death."

Doctor, I'm having trouble breathing!
Don't worry, we'll soon put a stop to that!

Do you know a bloke with one eye called Frank Jones?
No, what's his other eye called?

What do you get when you drop a piano down a mineshaft?
A flat miner!

A boy goes to a Doctor with an elephant on his head. "My word, you look like you need my help!" said the Doctor.
"You're telling me, Doc!"
said the elephant.
"Can you get this kid off my foot?"

Doctor, I have an awful lot of wind, can you give me anything for it?
Yes, you can borrow my kite!

The soldiers marched 50 miles to the battleground. As soon as they arrived, private Williams was shot. As he lay dying, he said to his mate, Bob, "I can't believe I marched all this way just to get shot!" "Yeah, but what about me?" said Bob,
"I've got to march all the way back again!"

Why is a tree like a dog?
Because they both lose their bark when they die!

A blind man went into a gift shop and started swinging his guide dog around his head on its lead. "Can I help you?" said the assistant.
"No thank you," said the blind man, "I'm just browsing."

An actor sawed off his own leg so he could play Long John Silver in a new movie.
He didn't get the part though...
it was the wrong leg!

Some Cannibal Munchies

Am I too late for dinner?
Yes, I'm afraid everyone's eaten!

Waiter: How many people for lunch?
Cannibal: Two each, please.

One cannibal to another:
I never met a man I didn't like!

What did the cannibal get when he was late for dinner?
The cold shoulder.

Did you hear about the cannibal who was expelled from school for buttering up his teacher?

Two cannibals were sitting by a fire. The first says, "Gee, I hate my mother-in-law."
The 2nd replies, "So, try the potatoes!"

A cannibal and his son are wandering through the desert and have not eaten in days. They come upon an oasis and decide to camp in the bushes till someone comes. The next morning they awake to see a beautiful woman bathing in the waterfall. As the father watches the lovely woman bathing, he is aware of his son at his side. The boy says, "I'm hungry dad, let's eat." The father replies,

"We can't eat her, she's gorgeous!" The boy grumbles that they have not eaten for days and he is really hungry. The father says he has a plan. The boy is overjoyed that he will soon eat, so he asks what the plan is...
The father says:
"We sneak up to the edge of the clearing, and when she comes out of the water, we kidnap her, take her home and eat your mother..."

What is a cannibal's favourite game?
Swallow the leader!

A tourist goes to Africa and asks his tourist guide, while walking in the jungle, "Are we safe here? Aren't there cannibals around?" And the tourist guide says, "You're completely safe. There are no cannibals in Africa." The tourist says, "How can you be sure?" And the tourist guide says: "We ate the last one on Monday!"

A cannibal goes into a restaurant. "How much for the set menu?" he asks. "Ten pounds a head," says the waiter. "Fine," says the cannibal, "I'll have a couple of arms and a foot as well."

Air Steward: Would you like to see the menu, Sir? Cannibal: No, just bring me the passenger list!

What do cats have for a breakfast?
Mice Krispies!

Tony's brother and his girlfriend shared the same birthday. He got his brother, a keen hunter, a new shotgun, and for his girlfriend a bottle of nice perfume. He wrote his girlfriend a sweet note saying "Use this on yourself and think of me." Unfortunately he put the note in with the wrong present...

Why did the mummy call the doctor? Because he was coffin!

Where did the vampire open his savings account? At a blood bank!

A man walks into a doctor's office. He has a cucumber up his nose, a carrot in his left ear and a banana in his right ear. "What's the matter with me?" he asks the doctor. The doctor replies, "You're not eating properly."

The Titanic is beginning to sink and everyone is abandoning ship. "Excuse me, Steward. Are there any sharks in the ocean here?" asks a little old lady, terrified.
"Yes, I'm afraid there are. But not to worry, we have a special gel in the bottle in your cabin especially for emergencies like this. Just rub the gel onto your arms and legs."
"And if I do this, the sharks won't eat me?" asks the little lady.
"Oh, they'll eat you all right, but they won't enjoy it nearly as much."

What did the skunk say when the wind changed direction?
"It's all coming back to me now!"

A boy is sitting on a train chewing gum and staring into space when the old lady opposite him says,
"It's no good talking to me, young man, I'm stone deaf!"

A young man from the city went to visit his farmer uncle. For the first few days, the uncle showed him the usual things - chickens, cows, crops, etc. After three days, however, it was obvious that the nephew was getting bored, and the uncle was running out of things to amuse him with. Finally, the uncle had an idea. "Why don't you grab a gun, take the dogs, and go hunting?" This seemed to cheer the nephew up, and with enthusiasm, off he went with the dogs. After a few hours, the nephew returned.
"How did you enjoy that?"
asked the uncle.
"It was great!" exclaimed the nephew.
"Got any more dogs?"

My wife and I tour theatres with our animal impressions act.
She does the sounds, I do the smells...

How does a monster count to 13?

On his fingers!

A tough old cowboy told his grandson that if he wanted to live a long life, the secret was to sprinkle a little gunpowder on his cornflakes every morning. The grandson did this every day and he lived to the age of 93. When he died, he left 14 children, 28 grandchildren, 35 great grandchildren and a 15-foot hole in the wall of the crematorium...

What do you call a man with a spade in his head? Doug!

What do you call a man without a spade in his head? Douglas!

Mummy! Why are we pushing the car off the cliff? Shut up, you'll wake your little brother!

No Dogs Allowed

A guy walking his Alsatian says to a guy walking his little Chihuahua, "Let's go over to that restaurant and get something to eat." The guy with the Chihuahua says, "We can't go in there. We've got dogs with us." The guy with the Alsatian says, "Just leave it to me." They go over to the restaurant, and the guy with the Alsatian puts on a pair of dark glasses, and walks in. A waiter says, "Sorry, sir, no pets allowed." The guy with the Alsatian says, "You don't understand, I'm blind, this is my guide dog!" The waiter says, "I'm terribly sorry, Sir. Come on in." The guy with the Chihuahua puts on a pair of dark glasses, and walks in. The waiter says, "I'm sorry, Sir. No pets allowed." "You don't understand," says the guy. "I'm blind, this is my guide dog!" The waiter says, "What, a Chihuahua?" Thinking quickly, the guy says, "Don't tell me they've given me a Chihuahua?!"

What do your call two robbers?
A pair of nickers!

What do you get if you cross a bear with a skunk?
Winnie-the-Pooh!

A man goes skydiving for the first time. After listening to the instructor for what seems like days, he is ready to go. Excited, he jumps out of the plane. About five seconds later, he pulls the ripcord. Nothing happens. He tries again. Still nothing. He starts to panic, but remembers his reserve chute. He pulls that cord. Nothing happens. He frantically begins pulling both cords, but to no avail. Suddenly, he looks down and he can't believe his eyes. Another man is in the air with him, but this guy is going up! Just as the other guy passes by, the skydiver yells,

"**Hey! Do you know anything about skydiving?**"
The other man shouts back,
"No! Do you know anything about gas cookers?"

Your Mum is so fat...

I ran around her twice and got lost!

I saw a picture of her in a magazine on page 4, 5, 6, 7, and 8!

Instead of Levi's 501 jeans, she wears Levi's 1002's!

She fell in the Grand Canyon and got wedged in!

She goes to a restaurant, looks at the menu, and says "Okay"!

She has to grease her hands to get into her pockets!

She has to put her belt on with a boomerang!

After she got off the Merry-Go-Round, the horse limped for a week!

When she was diagnosed with the flesh-eating disease the doctor gave her 13 years to live!

She puts mayonnaise on aspirins!

Her bottom has its own Member of Parliament!

Her cereal bowl came with a lifeguard!

When she goes to the zoo the elephants throw her peanuts!

Her school picture was an aerial photograph!

Her driving licence says, "Picture continued on the other side!"

They had to change "One size fits all"
to "One size fits most!"

When she gets in a lift, it HAS to go down!

People jog around her for exercise!

When she goes to a restaurant, she doesn't get a menu, she gets an estimate!

When they used her underwear elastic for bungee jumping, they hit the ground!

When I tried to drive around her, I ran out of petrol!

All the restaurants in town have signs that say: MAXIMUM OCCUPANCY: 240 PATRONS or YOUR MUM!

A picture of her fell off the wall!

She jumped up in the air and got stuck!

She was floating in the ocean and Spain claimed her as a New World!

She sat on a rowing machine and it sank!

A man gets pulled over by the police.
The officer walks up to car and says,
"Excuse me, Sir, but do you realise your
wife fell out of the car two miles back?"
"Thank Goodness for that," says the man,
"I thought I'd gone deaf!"

Ah, Doctor Watson.
You're wearing your winter underwear!
Good Lord, Holmes! How on Earth did
you deduce that?
You've forgotten to put
your trousers on again!

How do you get a zombie out of bed?
With a Hoover!

A guy is going on an ocean cruise,
and he tells his doctor that
he's worried about getting seasick.
The doctor says,
"Just eat two pounds of stewed tomatoes
before you leave the dock."

The guy says, "Will that keep me from getting sick, Doc?"
The doctor says,
"No, but it'll look very pretty in the water."

How did you burn your face?
At the Hallowe'en party,
I was bobbing for chips!

**Little Darren refused to eat. So his
mother took him to the Doctor.
The Doctor asked, "What would you like
to eat?" "A worm," Darren said.
Reluctantly, the Doc sent his
nurse out for a worm.
Placing it on a plate,
the Doc said, "Here it is."
"I want it fried," said the boy. The nurse
took it out and fried it. When she brought
it back, the Doc said, "Now eat it."
"I only want half and you eat the other
half," said Darren.
The Doctor swallowed one half
and gave the other to the boy.
Just then little Darren began to cry. The
doctor asked what was wrong.**
Darren said, "You ate my half!"

Little Johnny was in church with his mom for Sunday service when he suddenly felt sick. "Mum, I think I'm going to throw up!"
She told him, "I want you to run outside as fast as you can. Run across the lawn and go behind the bushes. You can throw up behind the bushes and nobody will see you." So Johnny ran for the door. Less than a minute later, he returned to his seat next to his mom. He had the look of obvious relief on his young face. "Did you make it all the way to the bushes, Johnny?"
"I didn't have to go that far, Mum. Just as I got to the front door, I found a box that had a sign on it that said 'FOR THE SICK'."

What do you call a deer with no eyes?
No idea!

What do you call a deer with no eyes and no legs?
Still no idea!

What do you get if you cross an owl with a skunk?
A bird that smells but doesn't give a hoot!

Why do worms taste like chewing gum?
Because they're Wrigleys!

What do you call a man with no arms and no legs who lives in a bush?
Russell!

A worried woman goes to the Doctor and asks him:
"Doctor, what can I do? My husband was asleep with his mouth open, and he's swallowed a mouse!"
"Calm down," said the Doctor. "It's quite simple, you must tie a piece of cheese to some string and dangle it over your husband's mouth. As soon as the mouse takes a bite, whip him out!"
"Right-ho Doctor, thank you. I'll just nip

round to the fishmonger for a cod's head,"
said the woman. "What?" said the Doc,
"What on Earth do you need a
cod's head for?"

"Oh, I forgot
to tell you,
I've got to
get the cat
out first!"

Where do you find giant snails?
At the end of giants' fingers!

A man is feeling very ill, so he goes to see his doctor and is immediately rushed to hospital to undergo tests. The man wakes up after the tests in a private room at the hospital, and the phone by his bed rings. "This is your doctor. We've had the results back from your tests and we've found you have a really nasty disease, and it's very catching."
"Oh my God, doctor! What are you going to do?"
"We're going to put you on a diet of pizzas, pancakes and pitta bread."
"Will that cure me?" said the man.
"Well no, but it's the only food we can get under the door!"

Doctor, I think I'm going to die!
Nonsense, that's the last thing you'll do!

The Speedy Turtle

A guy comes walking into a bar with a little turtle in his hand. The turtle's one eye is black and blue, two of his legs are bandaged, and his whole shell is taped together with sticky tape. The bartender asks the man, "What's wrong with your turtle?" "Nothing," the man responds. "This turtle is super fast! Take your dog and let him stand at the end of the bar. Then go and stand at the other end of the room and call your dog. I'll bet you £50 that before your dog reaches you, my turtle will be there." So the bartender, thinking it's an easy £50, agrees. He goes to the other side of the bar, and on the count of three calls his dog. Suddenly the guy picks up his turtle and throws it across the room, narrowly missing the bartender, and smashing into the wall. "Fifty pounds, please."

What do you call a man who was born in Manchester, married in London, and died in Glasgow?

Dead!

This man took his two-year-old daughter, Madison, to the DIY superstore. Madison got tired of walking, so he let her ride on his shoulders. As he walked, Madison began pulling his hair. Although he asked her to stop several times, she kept on. Getting annoyed, he scolded, "Madison! Stop that!"

"But, Daddy," she replied, "I'm just trying to get my chewing gum back!"

It was the last day of school and children brought gifts for the teachers. The flower shop owner's son brought a big bouquet of flowers for Miss Jones. The candy store owner's daughter

brought her a big box of chocolates. The off-licence owner's son brought a big heavy box. The teacher lifted the box and noticed it was leaking. She tasted one of the drops.
"Oo, is it wine?" she guessed.
"Nooo..," said the little boy.
She tasted another drop.
"Is it Champagne?"
she guessed.
"Nooo..," said the little boy.
"I give up." she said,
"What is it?"
"It's a puppy, Miss!"

A man is sitting at home one night. Suddenly, there's a loud knock at the door. The man opens the door to find a six-foot beetle standing at the doorstep. "What in the world is this?" he asks. The beetle responds by attacking the man viciously, with a flurry of kicks and punches. Then the beetle leaves. The man crawls into his house and calls an ambulance. At the hospital, the nurse asks him how it happened. The guy tells her about the beetle and what happened. "Yes," the nurse says, with an understanding nod, "there is a nasty bug going around at the moment..."

What's green, hairy and takes Aspirin?
A gooseberry with a hangover!

What's the best time to pick apples?
When the farmer's not looking!

In a hospital, a man wakes up from surgery.
Man: How did it go, Doctor?
Doctor: Well, the bad news is we've had to amputate both your legs...
Man: Oh no! What's the good news?
Doctor: The man in the next bed wants to buy your slippers!

How did the dentist become a brain surgeon?
When his drill slipped!

"Look at the speed of that thing!" said one hawk to another as a jet flew past.
"Not really surprising," said the second.
"You'd fly that fast if your bum was on fire!"

Teacher: Sara, if you had 16 chocolates, and Charlie asked you for ten, how many would you have left?
Sara: Sixteen, I hate Charlie.

Why did the basketball floor get wet?
The players dribbled on it!

There was a bloke on a motorcycle driving down the road on a cold and windy day. After a while he decided to put his leather jacket on backwards to protect him better against the wind. Five minutes later he took a corner too fast, hit a patch of oil on the road and crashed the bike. A passer-by found him, called the police and told them what happened. The police asked him, "Is he showing any signs of life?" The passer-by then said, "Well, he was till I turned his head around the right way."

The first cannibal asked the second cannibal, "Aren't you done eating yet?" The second cannibal replied, "I'm on my last leg now!"

1st man: Every day I go for a tramp in the woods with my dog.
2nd man: I bet the dog enjoys that!
1st man: He does:
the tramp's getting a bit
fed up, though!

The Speed Cop

A farmer got pulled over by a policeman for speeding. The cop gave the farmer a big lecture about how stupid he was. Finally, he wrote out the ticket, and as he was doing that he kept swatting at some flies buzzing around his head. The farmer said, "Having some problems with circle flies there?" The cop stopped and said, "Circle flies? Never heard of them!" So the farmer says, "Well, they're called circle flies because they circle around the back end of a horse." The cop says, "Oh," and goes back to writing the ticket. After a minute he stops and says, "Hey...wait a minute, are you trying to call me a horse's arse?" The farmer says, "Oh no, officer. I wouldn't even think that!" The cop says, "Well, alright then," and goes back to writing the ticket. After a pause, the farmer says:

"Can't fool those flies though."

A blind beggar says to a passing woman, "Excuse me, love. Can you spare a pound for a blind man?" The woman looks at him suspiciously. "Wait a minute, I'm sure you can see out of that eye!"

"Alright," he says, "Give me 50 pence, then."

Joe comes home to his wife very upset. "The Doctor told me I've got to take these pills for the rest of my life," he tells her. "So, what's the problem?" she asks.

"He only gave me six!"

What's the difference between Tony Blair and a dog?

Tony Blair usually wears a suit, a dog just pants!

Mother: Mrs Jokes next door has a new baby.

Daughter: What will she do with her old one?

A salesman is getting the sack from his boss for being useless at his job. "Give me one more chance," he pleads, "I'll sell anything!" His boss gives him a hundred toothbrushes and tells him if he sells them all in an hour, he can keep his job. In an hour's time, the salesman is back with a bundle of money. His boss is amazed... "How on Earth did you manage to sell all those toothbrushes?" The man says, "Well, I stood on a street corner with a plate of toast and spread, and gave pieces away free. People would try a bite of toast and say "Yuck! That tastes like dog poo!" And I'd say, "It is! Do you want to buy a toothbrush?"

What is green and has four legs and two trunks?
Two seasick tourists!

How do you tidy up a murder scene?
With a victim cleaner!

A woman got on a bus holding a baby. The bus driver said: "Blimey! that's the ugliest baby I've ever seen!" In a huff, the woman slammed her fare into the tray and took a seat near the back of the bus. The man sitting next to her sensed that she was upset and asked her what was wrong. "The bus driver completely insulted me!" she fumed. The man said, "He can't do that, he's a public servant. He's not allowed to say things to insult passengers!"

"You're right," she said. "I think I'll go back up there and give him a piece of my mind."

"That's a good idea," the man said. "Here, let me hold your monkey..."

What happened to the man who couldn't keep up payments to his exorcist? He was repossessed!

A young woman smashes her car into a lamp post, and the police are gathering details about the accident.

Policeman: Can you tell me what gear you were in, Miss?

Young Lady: Yes, I was wearing white jeans and a cut-off T-shirt...

Did you hear about the two peanuts that were walking down the street and one got beaten up?
Yes, he was a salted!

A little boy watched, fascinated, as his mother gently rubbed cold cream on her face. "Why are you rubbing cold cream on you face, mommy?" he asked. "To make myself beautiful," said his mother. A few minutes later, she began removing the cream with a tissue.
"What's the matter?" he asked.
"Are you giving up?

A bear and a rabbit are taking a dump in the woods. The bear turns to the rabbit and says, "Hey, do have a problem with it, you know, sticking to your fur?" The rabbit says, "Nope, never."
So the bear wipes his bum
with the rabbit...

What's better than a drip dry vampire?
A wash and werewolf!

A man walks into a restaurant with a shark. "Do you serve children in here?" he askes the barman. "Certainly, Sir," the barman replies.
"Good. A pizza for me, then, please, and two children for the shark..."

How do you make holy water?
Boil the hell out of it!

Why was the Egyptian girl worried?
Because her daddy was a mummy!

Postman 1: A dog bit me on the leg this morning.
Postman 2: Did you put anything on it?
Postman 1: No, he seemed to like it plain!

How do you keep a skunk from smelling?
Hold his nose!

What's a haunted chicken?
A poultry-geist!

A circus owner walked into a bar to see everyone crowded about a table watching a little show. On the table was an upside-down pot and a duck dancing on it. The circus owner was so impressed that he offered to buy the duck from its owner. After some wheeling and dealing they settled for $10,000 for the duck and the pot. Three days later the circus owner runs back to the bar in anger: "Your duck is a rip-off! I put him on the pot before a whole audience and he didn't dance a single step!" "Well," said the duck's former owner,
"did you remember to light a candle under the pot?"

Where do mummies go for a swim?
To the Dead Sea!

Why do witches fly around on broomsticks?
Because Hoovers don't have long
enough cords!!

A man finds he hasn't been able to go to the toilet for three days and he goes to the Doctor to do something about it. The Doc gives him a laxative and sends him home, telling him to take it at midnight. Next day, the man calls the Doctor on the phone: "Doc, that laxative you gave me really did the trick, I took it at midnight and I went at 8 o' clock this morning!" "Yep," says the Doc, "works in 8 hours, guaranteed!" "That's the problem," says the man, "I didn't wake up till half past nine..."

"Doctor, will this ointment clear up my itchy spots?"
"I'm not making any rash promises!"

A guy goes in to see a psychiatrist. He says,
"Doc, I can't seem to make any friends. Can you help me, you fat slob?"

The Almond Bowl

A vicar decides one day to visit one of his elderly parishoners, Mrs Smith. He rings the door bell and Mrs Smith appears. "Good Day Mrs Smith. I just thought I would drop by and see how you're getting on." The woman says, "Oh I'm fine, Vicar, come on in and we'll have some tea." While sitting at the coffee table, the vicar notices a bowl of almonds on the table. "Mind if I have one?" the vicar says. "Not at all, have as many as you like." After a few hours the vicar looks at his watch and, alarmed at how long he has been visiting, says to Mrs Smith, "Oh my goodness, look at the time! I must be going. Oh but, dear me, I have eaten all your almonds. I'll have to replace them next time I visit!" To which Mrs Smith replied,

"Oh don't bother Father.
Ever since I lost all my teeth, it's all I can do just to lick the chocolate off them."

"Mommy, my turtle is dead," wailed the little boy to his mother, holding the turtle out to her in his hand. His Mum said, "That's all right. We'll wrap him in tissue paper, put him in a little box, then have a lovely burial ceremony in the back yard. After that, we'll go out for a yummy big ice cream, and then get you a great new pet, like a puppy! Just then, she noticed the turtle move. "Look! Your turtle isn't dead after all!" "Oh," said the boy, "can we kill it?"

Bobby says to the gardener: "What are you doing with that manure?" The gardener says: "I'm putting it on my rhubarb." "Really?" says Bobby. "We usually have custard on ours!"

How do you teach a dog to fetch? Tie a cat to a stick!

Mum, Can I have a dog for Christmas?

No, you can have turkey like everyone else!

The Children's Party

A lady is giving a party for her grand-daughter, and has hired a clown. Just before the party starts, two tramps turn up at the door. The woman tells them that she'll pay them to chop some wood for her. Gratefully, they head to the back of the house... All is going well, with the kids having a wonderful time, but the clown phones to cancel! The woman is very disappointed; she happens to look out the window and sees one of the tramps doing cartwheels across the lawn and yodelling. She watches amazed as he swings from branches, does mid-air flips, and leaps in the air. She says to the other tramp, "Do you think your friend would do that again for the children? I would pay him £50!" The tramp says, "I dunno. I'll ask him... Hey, Willie, for fifty quid, would you chop off another toe?"

What do you call a person who puts poison in a person's corn flakes?
A cereal killer!

What do you call four drowning bullfighters?
Quattro sinko!

How did the carpenter break his teeth?
He chewed his nails!

Jack: Did you hear about the giant that threw up?
Jill: No, how'd you know?
Jack: It's all over town!

A man takes his Rottweiler to the vet. "My dog's cross-eyed, is there anything you can do for him?" "Alright," says the vet, "let's have a look at him." So he picks the dog up and has a good look at its eyes. "Well," says the vet, "I'm afraid I'm going to have to put him down." "Why? Because he's cross-eyed?"
"No, because he's extremely heavy..."

A family of moles had been hibernating all winter. One beautiful spring morning, they woke up. The father mole stuck his head out of the hole and looked around. "Mother Mole!" he called back down the hole. "Come up here! I smell honey, freshly-made honey!"

The mother mole ran up and squeezed in next to him. "That's not honey, that's maple syrup! I smell maple syrup!" The baby mole, still down in the hole, was sulking.

"I can't smell anything down here but molasses...."

Mummy. I hate my sister's guts!
You'll eat what's put in front of you!

Diner: Waiter? I can't eat this chicken. Call the manager.
Waiter: It's no use.
He can't eat it either!

Did you hear about the cannibal policeman who was arrested?
He was caught grilling his suspects!

Bigger in Texas

This man decided to visit Texas. When he arrived on the plane, he saw the seats and said, "Wow, these seats are big!" The person next to him said, "Everything is big in Texas." When he got to Texas, he decided to visit a bar. He ordered a beer and got a mug placed in his hand. He exclaimed, "Wow these mugs are big!" The barman said, "Everything is big in Texas." After ten more beers, the man asked the barman where the toilets were.. The barman replied, "Second door to the right." The man staggered to his feet and headed for the loo, but accidentally tripped over and skipped the second door. Instead, he entered the third door, which lead to the swimming pool. He crashed through it and fell into the pool by accident. Scared to death, the man started shouting, "Don't flush, don't flush!"

Your Sister is so Ugly...

When she joined an ugly contest, they said "Sorry, no professionals!"

She looked out the window and got arrested for mooning!

When she was born, your Mum said, "What a treasure!" and your Dad said, "Yes, let's bury it!"

When she goes to the bank, they turn off the surveillance cameras!

You have to tie a sausage around her neck to get the dog to play with her!

The government moved Hallowe'en to her birthday!

She threw a boomerang and it wouldn't even come back!

When she sits in the sand on the beach, cats try to bury her!

Your Dad takes her to work with him so that he doesn't have to kiss her goodbye!

Her dentist treats her by mail-order!

Her pillow cries at night!

If she was a scarecrow, the potatoes would run away!

People hang her picture in their cars so their radios don't get stolen!

She looks like her face caught fire and they put it out with a fork!

She tried to take a bath and the water jumped out!

When she was born, the doctor smacked the wrong end!

When she was a baby, her parents had to feed her with a catapault!

She made an onion cry!

An old chap and his little grandson Eddy were digging for fishing bait in the garden. Uncovering a many-legged creature, Eddy proudly dangled it before his Grandad. "No, Ed, he won't do for bait," his Grandad said. "He's not an earthworm."
"He's not?" Eddy asked. "What planet is he from?"

Why did the lion throw up after he'd eaten the priest?
Because it's hard to keep a good man down!

A man is standing at a bus stop eating sausage and chips when a woman turns up with a dog. The dog is very excited at the smell of sausage and starts barking like crazy. "Shall I throw him a bit?" says the man. "If you like," says the woman.
So he chucked the dog over a wall...

What did one zombie ask the other?
Can you lend me a hand?

The Rude Parrot

A lady goes to a pet shop one day and buys a talking parrot. As soon as she gets it home, the parrot says "What a dump! This place sucks! You should get the hoover out once in a while, you lazy old bat!" The lady is shocked. "How dare you be so rude!" she says, and she puts the parrot in a cupboard to teach it a lesson. An hour later, she takes it out. "Are you going to behave?" she asks. "Get stuffed you old crow!" says the parrot. "How dare you be so rude!" says the lady, and she stuffs the parrot into a saucepan, to teach it a lesson. An hour later, she takes it out again. "Well, are you going to be nice now?" she asks it. "Go and boil your head, you wrinkly old cow!" said the parrot. "How dare you be so rude!" says the lady, and she sticks the parrot in the freezer, to teach it a lesson once and for all. An hour later she takes it out.

"Are you going to behave?" she asks.

The parrot shivers, "Y-Yes, Miss, I'm going to be g-good from now on, th-thank you very m-much." Sure enough, he is good as gold all afternoon.

That evening, the lady is putting the cover over the cage for the night when the parrot says in a little voice,

"By the way, just how rude was that chicken?"

Did you hear about the constipated Maths teacher?

He worked it out with a pencil!

The farmer says to his wife, "Two of our hens have stopped laying." "How do you know?" says his wife.

"Because I've just run them over with a tractor."

What does the Queen do when she burps?

Issues a royal pardon!

Pam: Is it OK to eat hotdogs with hands?
Sam: No, hotdogs aren't supposed to have hands!

What's big and green and slimy, and hangs from tall trees?
Elephant bogies!

What did one zombie say to another?
Get a life!

Why do monkeys scratch themselves?
Because they're the only ones who know where the itch is!

Farmer John: That pig is like one of the family.
Farmer Bob: Really? Which one?

What happened when a cannibal went on a self-catering holiday?
He ate himself!

Why are Giraffes' necks so long?
Because their feet stink!

A very old man is sitting on a bench in tears. A lady goes up to him and asks "Excuse me. But is something wrong?" "It's my 100th birthday today," said the old man. "I've got lots of friends coming round to my house with champagne and cake. There'll be a band playing music and they've hired dancing girls to entertain me, and everyone's bought me lots of wonderful gifts." "Well, that sounds marvellous," said the lady. "Why are you upset, then?" The old chap looked up and wailed: "I can't remember where I live!"

Why do ghouls and demons hang out together?
Because demons are a ghoul's best friend!

What do you call a man with rabbits in his trousers?
Warren!

Young Marie went to visit her cousin
Sophie in France. She was most excited
about learning French. When she arrived, she
was even more thrilled because Sophie's
cat had just had a kitten, and Sophie gave
it to Marie to raise as her very own. Because
Marie was beginning to learn French, she
named her new kitten Un Deux Trois.
One day, Marie and Sophie were playing
beside the river. Marie put her kitten in a
small toy boat and pulled it along the river.
Unfortunately, a large boat sped by, and the
wake tipped Marie's toy boat and the kitten
spilled overboard. Seeing Marie in tears,
Sophie rushed up and asked what
had happened.

Marie said, "Un Deux Trois cat sank!"

**Why did the Mexican throw his wife out
of the window?**

He wanted tequila!

**How do you catch an elephant?
Dig a hole, fill it with ashes,
surround it by peas.**
When he comes to take a pea, kick
him in the ash hole!

Why do surgeons wear masks?
If somebody makes a mistake nobody
will know who did it!

**Which hand do you use to clean the
toilet? My right hand.**
Really! I'd use a brush!

How do you make a cat go "woof"?
Set him on fire!

**Two men meet on a train.
One asks after the other's wife.
"Oh, she's dead..," says the friend.
"She was chopping french beans and
accidentally cut her own head clean off."**

**"Good Lord!" says the other chap.
"What did you do?"**
"What else could I do?
I opened a tin of peas..."

Strangers in a Bar

A couple of strangers were drinking at a cliffside bar overlooking the ocean. Both of them are a little drunk, when one says to the other: "Hey, look at the wind whipping up the side of that cliff. I'll bet I could jump off of the ledge, catch the wind in my coat, and get lifted right back up to the bar!" "No way," says the other guy, "you'd fall to your death." "Well, I'm going to try it!" says the first, and at that he walks over, stands on the ledge, and leaps off in a dive. Sure enough, he comes sailing back up, and lands on his feet in front of the bar. "I can't believe it!" says the second guy, "That's impossible." So the first drunk does it again: he jumps off the cliff, catches the wind in his coat, and comes sailing back to the bar. "Go ahead," he says, "try it, it's great!" "Well, OK, I'm just drunk enough to give it a go," says the second fellow.

So he climbs the ledge and leaps off the cliff, only to fall screaming to his death on the rocks below.

The first guy walks back to the bar and sits down to his drink.

The bartender steps over, looks him in the eye, and says to him:

"You know, you can be really mean sometimes when you've been drinking, Superman."

Grandad: Look at my fantastic new hearing aid, it's made with the very latest technology developed from the US Space programme.

Grandson: Wow! How does it work?

Grandad: Half past seven!

Why did the lady miss her husband?

Because she never shot a gun before!

What happens if you upset a cannibal?

You get into hot water!

Little Johnny is approached by the lifeguard at the public swimming pool. "You're not allowed to wee in the pool," said the lifeguard. "I'm going to report you." "But everyone wees in the pool," said Little Johnny.
"Possibly," said the lifeguard, "but not from the diving board!"

A man is walking by a children's playground and hears all the kids chanting, "Thirteen! Thirteen! Thirteen!" Quite curious about all this, he finds a hole in the fence, looks in and someone pokes him in the eye. Everyone in the playground starts chanting,
"Fourteen! Fourteen! Fourteen!"

What do you get if you cross a skeleton and a dog?
An animal that buries itself in the garden!